Concerning Spiritual Gifts

Concerning Spiritual Gifts

NOW CONCERNING SPIRITUAL GIFTS, BRETHREN, I WOULD NOT HAVE YOU

IGNORANT. 1 COR. 12:1

DR. EDWARD J. HEARNS

Adullam Bible College

CONCERNING SPIRITUAL GIFTS

Adullam Bible College Press
In association with Serious Season Press

©2017 by Edward J. Hearns
ISBN 13: 978-1946909008

Cover Design by Erica D. Hearns

For information regarding ordering, bulk purchases, or other inquiries, please contact Adullam Bible College at Adullamcollege@gmail.com

Contents

Part V: Ministry Gifts

"I Would Not Have You Ignorant"

Now, concerning spiritual gifts, brethren, I would not have you ignorant. I Cor. 12:1

This book was written to give inside information to men and women about the gifts the Lord gave to the church. My inspiration was to clear up some of the myths and mystery concerning the gifts of the Spirit. Some people see the gifts as too mystical or out of place in today's church. Others believe they are only given to those more qualified or in a higher office than themselves. No matter your position on the subject, I believe you will find the information contained in this book informative and enlightening.

There is no time or age when the gifts were not needed or did not operate in the church. Even before the church age there is evidence of the gifts operating within and on behalf of mankind.

Not all gifts belong to the Supernatural realm. Some seek to be used in this realm because they desire to be seen as powerful; some who do not possess supernatural gifts see their lack as confirmation God has no purpose for them in the kingdom. Both of these mindsets display a lack of understanding.

The gifts of the Holy Spirit are not designed to bring attention to oneself, but to bring glory and honor to God. God not using you in the supernatural does not imply He has no use for you in ministry. Whether you are in a ministry consisting of five or five thousand, one truth will remain the same: there will be more people being used who are not seen than who are seen.

> [8]For to one is given by the Spirit the word of wisdom; to another the word of knowledge by the same Spirit; [9]To another faith by the same Spirit; to another the gifts of healing by the same Spirit; [10]To another the working of miracles; to another prophecy; to another discerning of spirits; to another *divers* kinds of tongues; to another the interpretation of tongues: I Cor. 12:8-10

The gifts listed above are most commonly referred to as the supernatural gifts of the Holy Spirit. When you hear someone speaking or teaching on the gifts of the Spirit, this is the text a large percentage will teach from. It is a good place to start, but one must remember the supernatural gifts only represent one portion of the gifts the Holy Spirit gave to the church. Although they were given to all the churches, you will find them most in operation in the charismatic or Pentecostal denominations.

Everyone has a gift, but not everyone will experience the supernatural aspects of the gifts listed above. Many are drawn to the church by these gifts. Others are repelled by the church because they don't believe in these gifts. Still others feel alienated from the church because they are not flowing in one of these gifts.

One who isn't operating in one of the supernatural gifts of the Spirit shouldn't be discouraged. God has given many gifts to the church which don't require one to be a spiritual giant but are a blessing to the body. One of the first lessons to be learned by one who desires to be used of God is the gift doesn't make you special. In fact, the gift has nothing to do with you. You don't have to be in a special realm or hold a special office.

As you dig into this study, you will find the operations of some gifts are more closely related than others. This study separates the gifts into categories to aid you in examining those closely related in operation and administration together.

All the gifts work in concert with each other like the instruments in an orchestra. Although the instruments are separated into groups of woodwinds and brass, it is when they are combined they create a symphony.

PART I:
Gifts of Utterance

The ability to speak and communicate thoughts and ideas connects man to God in a way no other species on earth experiences. When God created the world, He simply spoke and the word spoken from His mouth framed the world and everything in it. The same power is available to us to speak our world into existence through the power of the tongue. Like God, man is a speaking spirit; also like God, man is able to change his world with the words of his mouth.

Since so much authority is given to the tongue, an entire division of the gifts of the Spirit is expressed through the tongue. These gifts are referred to as gifts of utterance. The gifts of utterance utilize the spoken word. The gifts are uttered by the tongues of men. They are speaking gifts. They represent the effect the spoken word has on men and women when the word is impacted by the Spirit of God. The gifts of utterance include tongues, interpretation of tongues, and prophecy.

CHAPTER ONE

Tongues

Tongues (glossolalia) is the supernatural ability to speak in an unknown language. This could be a language foreign to the person speaking or a heavenly language.

The gift of tongues is often considered the initial evidence of being filled with the Spirit in Pentecostal denominations. When the believer experiences the baptism of the Holy Spirit, this is evidenced by speaking in an unknown language:

> And they were all filled with the Holy Ghost, and began to speak with other tongues, as the Spirit gave them utterance. Acts 2:4

On the day of Pentecost, the believers were gathered together in anticipation of the "promise of the Father." It is obvious from their reaction, the apostles were expectant but ignorant to the nature of the gift to come. Like children expecting a gift from their Father, they were hopeful but unsure what they would receive. This is the state the apostles found themselves in on the day of Pentecost.

This had to be an especially trying time for the apostles. It was the heart of a festive season. All the time they were waiting, others were celebrating and feasting. After the feast of weeks came the last celebration, the day of Pentecost. Pentecost represented the 50th day of celebration. While others were eating and enjoying this festive day, the disciples were praying.

> 2And suddenly there came a sound from heaven as of a rushing mighty wind, and it filled all the house where they were sitting. 3And there appeared unto them cloven tongues like as of fire, and it sat upon each of them. 4And they were all filled with the Holy Ghost, and began to speak with other tongues, as the Spirit gave them utterance. Acts 2:2-4

This was the grand entrance of the Holy Spirit. First there was a sound then there was the appearance of tongues of fire. As they were filled with the Holy Spirit, they began speaking in other tongues.

This is a phenomenal day as the Apostles became eye witnesses to something which had never been experienced prior to this day in the earth realm. Not only did they witness the power of God, but they became active participants in the move of God when they opened their mouths and began to speak in an unknown language.

It could be argued this was the last time the gift of tongues would be accepted by all believers. Since the day of Pentecost, speaking in unknown tongues has been accepted as evidence one has experienced the baptism of the Holy Spirit. There were no denominations or established dogmas to dispute or attempt to control the move of God. There were only men who had obediently waited for the promise of the Father. When the Spirit moved and the tongues came, they were accepted as coming from God even though this display was not fully comprehended by those who experienced and witnessed it.

None of the gifts of the Spirit are surrounded by as much controversy as the gift of tongues. It could be argued this was the last time the gift of tongues would be accepted by all believers. Some denominations believe the gift of tongues was only given to the disciples on the day of Pentecost for a sign. By the same token other denominations believe you are not filled with the Holy Spirit unless you speak in tongues. As with most extreme beliefs, the truth can be found somewhere in the middle.

One can deduce several reasons why the gift of tongues was given to the church from scripture. The most obvious reason this gift was given was for a sign.

> [21]In the law it is written, With *men* of other tongues and other lips will I speak unto this people; and yet for all that will they not hear me, saith the Lord. [22]Wherefore tongues are for a sign, not to them that believe, but to them that believe not: but prophesying *serveth* not for them that believe not, but for them

which believe. I Cor. 14:21-22

The apostle Paul is referencing a scripture recorded by the prophet Isaiah. This scripture makes it abundantly clear tongues were given to the church for a sign. This is a supernatural ability only God can give to the believer. This is one of the reasons many believers accept the gift of tongues as a sign one has truly been filled with the Holy Spirit.

By the time Paul wrote this letter, the gift of tongues was already a hotly disputed gift and one which had grown out of control in the church. This letter was not written to strip the gift of tongues from the church, but rather to position it to bring unity instead of division.

Another clear reason why tongues were given to the church was for edification.

> He that speaketh in an unknown tongue edifieth himself; but he that prophesieth edifieth the church. I Cor. 14:4

Paul is writing to the church in Corinth to bring order to the church in his office as an apostle. He asserts the gift of tongues provides edification to the believer who prays in tongues. Although this scripture primarily expresses the value of prophesy, it is evident the gift of tongues is useful for the edification of oneself. Jude further expresses this same sentiment in his epistle:

> But ye, beloved, building up yourselves on your most

holy faith, praying in the Holy Ghost. Jude 1:20

The arguments made by some denominations attempt to devalue this gift as not essential in today's church, yet all of us need encouragement from time to time. If the gift of tongues serves as a source of encouragement and spiritual strength, it is just as necessary today as it was on the day of Pentecost.

CHAPTER TWO
Interpretation of Tongues

The gift of interpretation works alongside the gift of tongues. There are two administrations of the gift of interpretation of tongues: interpreting what is being said when someone is speaking in a foreign language, and; the ability to interpret the message being conveyed when someone is speaking in a heavenly language.

If someone is speaking in a foreign language and someone interprets what is being said, this can be confirmed by others who also speak the same language. This is what occurred on the day of Pentecost:

> [7]And they were all amazed and marvelled, saying one to another, Behold, are not all these which speak Galilaeans? [8]And how hear we every man in our own tongue, wherein we were born? Acts 2:7-8

Several conclusions can be drawn from the statement above. First, there's no doubt the men who are speaking are a different nationality and language than the ones listening. This is also evidence the listeners are not all from the same country.

Sometimes people try to belittle the supernatural aspects of the gifts of the Spirit to make it conform to their understanding. It is easy to dismiss the gift of interpretation as simply an ability to speak a foreign language. Although this makes it comfortable for people to understand, if this was all there was to it, it still wouldn't explain the phenomenon on the day of Pentecost.

One can get into trouble spiritually when one tries to make the supernatural gifts of the Holy Spirit behave naturally. Those who choose to believe the gift of interpretation is limited to interpreting what is said in foreign language allow for no discourse in heavenly or angelic tongues.

As soon as one gets comfortable believing this, they're hit between the eyes with another uncomfortable truth about the day of Pentecost. This event can only be explained naturally if all the other men spoke the same foreign language. The supernatural aspects of the gift is made manifest by the fact all the men from different countries simultaneously heard what was said in their own language. By natural means this is impossible. Trying to make supernatural gifts conform to the natural realm is ludicrous in intent and expression.

The last aspect of this gift is the one subject to the most controversy: to interpret a message given to the church in an unknown language. This controversy springs from this idea man ought to be able to explain supernatural things naturally. Before the day of Pentecost, there is no indication of the gift of tongues and interpretation in operation. Because of this, some still believe it was a one-time occurrence, similar to spanking the bottom of a baby when it's born. This idea is more appealing to one's reasoning because it allows one to categorize the gift and move on. The apostle Paul spent a large portion of the fourteenth chapter of First Corinthians addressing this gift and its operation in the body:

> Wherefore let him that speaketh in an unknown tongue pray that he may interpret. I Corinthians 14:13.

By the time this letter is written to the Corinthian church, the use of gifts had degenerated to the point the people were using them to exalt the gifted person and make themselves appear more spiritual. Paul used his apostolic office to bring order to the church so the gifts could be used in the manner for which they were given to the body. In the scripture above, Paul alludes to the fact the gifts operate in concert with one another. The gift of tongues alone would edify the individual believer but do nothing for the body. When tongues are used in concert with interpretation, the body is edified.

The gift of interpretation of tongues is co-dependent on the gift of tongues. If there were no tongues, there would be no need to interpret. In the same manner, without the interpretation of tongues, tongues would be mere babbling which would disturb rather than edify. These gifts complement each other so well, Paul encourages the believer who has the gift of tongues to pray for interpretation so the church may be edified.

What is the primary benefit of the gift of interpretation of tongues? The gift of interpretation promotes the gift of tongues so it is no longer only a benefit to the individual believer, but edifies the body of believers.

> For he that speaketh in an unknown tongue speaketh not unto men, but unto God: for no man understandeth him; howbeit in the spirit he speaketh mysteries. 1 Cor. 14:2

The Spirit reveals mysteries to the believer speaking in tongues. When you add the gift of interpretation, the veil is removed and the mysteries are shared with the entire congregation. Since the gift of tongues is given to the believers for edification, it is natural to assume what the Spirit reveals to one believer has the potential to encourage the whole body of believers.

Having the gift of interpretation of tongues is like having a personal translator. It is useful when a message is being conveyed in tongues, but otherwise it is not needed. It is like having an employee who speaks Spanish. If you don't deal with Spanish speaking customers every day, there will be times you won't need him to perform this task. At the times you do have a Spanish speaking customer, this employee is invaluable. He would be the only link between you and Spanish speaking customers. To deal with this situation you would have to: 1) Retain the Spanish speaking employee, or 2) Refuse to serve the Spanish speaking customers.

Unfortunately many churches have chosen the second option. Instead of praying for an interpreter, they have told the believer speaking in tongue to refrain. As our churches become more intellectually driven, these precious gifts are becoming dormant in the church.

CHAPTER THREE
Prophecy

The gift of prophecy is one of the most coveted gifts in the body. When one has the gift of prophecy, there are times it seems one is given inside information unavailable to everyone else. The apostle Paul spoke of the importance of prophecy in the body of Christ:

> I would that ye all spake with tongues but rather that ye prophesied: for greater is he that prophesieth than he that speaketh with tongues, except he interpret, that the church may receive edifying. I Cor. 14:5

Like all gifts, the gift of prophecy is given to the body for edification. When Paul says he who prophesies is greater, it doesn't mean the person or the gift is greater; it means prophecy has a greater effect on more people. Unlike when a person is speaking in tongues, when someone is prophesying, others are able to hear and judge the prophecy.

Prophecy is not limited to foretelling upcoming events. It also consists of inspired preaching which edifies. Oftentimes when someone is preaching under the gift of prophecy, it will seem as if they were with you before the service. You will find yourself making comments like "I was just talking to someone about that today", or "I'm going through the same thing right now".

> But he that prophesieth speaketh unto men to edification, and exhortation, and comfort. I Cor. 14:3

The gift of prophecy reveals a word in season. Prophecy elevates ordinary preaching to a level which impacts the lives of men in a way only God can. Through prophecy men have not only heard from men; they have heard from God.

Prophecy also has the added benefit of revealing the secrets of hearts. It is through the gift of prophecy the word of God is able to pierce the veil of man's heart and reveal his innermost secrets:

> 24But if all prophesy, and there come in one that believeth not, or *one* unlearned, he is convinced of all, he is judged of all: 25And thus are the secrets of his heart made manifest; and so falling down on *his* face he will worship God, and report that God is in you of a truth. I Cor. 14:24-25

The gift of prophecy is not intended to be a vehicle to draw attention to men or cause one to be puffed up; it is a means of drawing attention to the Spirit of God. When it is used in the correct way, one realizes God Himself is revealing secrets only He can divulge.

Since prophecy is such an amazing gift, it is often the most sought after, and usually for the wrong reasons. Some people want to be used in the prophetic to be able to demonstrate to others how wonderful they are. When used out of a desire to be seen or thought of as special, the gift of prophecy is easily perverted by the enemy. It opens the door for a spirit of pride. Those who walk in the prophetic must always walk in humility to avoid the many pitfalls of the enemy. This will be discussed more when the office of the prophet is examined.

PART II:
Gifts of Revelation

It is not expedient for me doubtless to glory. I will come to visions and revelations of the Lord. I Corinthians 12:2

Gifts of revelation are gifts which reveal spiritual truths only God can impart to man. Revelations are an uncovering of what is hidden or unseen. The gifts of revelation reveal the hidden things of the spirit.

There is a spiritual realm which transcends the world one experiences every day. The spiritual realm is not accessible to everyone and because of this, it is easy to dismiss or relegate it to the fancy of people who lack understanding and foolishly accept everything the Bible says at face value.

If one dismisses the gifts of revelation because one doesn't understand them, one is in fact dismissing part of the word of God.

No matter how hard you try, you will never be able to make everything in the word of God make sense to the carnal mind. This is where it gets messy and you lose a lot of well-meaning people. Paul lets us know the carnal man has a problem understanding the things of the Spirit:

> But the natural man receiveth not the things of the Spirit of God: for they are foolishness unto him: neither can he know them, because they are spiritually discerned. I Cor. 2:14

If you are to understand the gifts of revelation, you must understand them from a spiritual perspective. There are three gifts in this category: the word of wisdom, the word of knowledge, and discerning of spirits. In this section, these gifts will be carefully examined and examples of them in the Old and New Testament will be highlighted to expand your understanding of their use.

CHAPTER FOUR
The Word of Wisdom

The word of wisdom can best be described as the supernatural revelation of upcoming events. The prophet Amos states it this way:

> Surely the Lord GOD will do nothing, but he revealeth his secret unto his servants the prophets. Amos 3:7

God reveals secrets to the prophets. Sometimes these secrets come as a word of wisdom.

The apostle Paul used the word of wisdom to warn sailors of upcoming disaster in the book of Acts.

> [22]And now I exhort you to be of good cheer: for there shall be no loss of any man's life among you, but of the ship. [23]For there stood by me this night the angel of God, whose I am, and whom I serve, [24]Saying, Fear not, Paul; thou must be brought before Caesar: and, lo, God hath given thee all them that sail with thee. [25]Wherefore, sirs, be of good cheer: for I believe God,

that it shall be even as it was told me. Acts 27:22-25

Paul was given a word of wisdom by an angelic messenger who revealed the fate of the ship they were sailing on. Because of this word, he was able to comfort and encourage those who were sailing with him in the face of an impending storm. The storm would wreak havoc and destroy the ship, but leave all the men alive.

This is an excellent example of the operation of the word of wisdom. If you read the entire chapter, you will find Paul doesn't only give them this word after they set sail. He tried to warn them of the coming storm before they set sail. However, they chose not to heed his warning.

The gift of God is also a reflection of the grace of God. Even though the men did not heed the warning given the first time, God still uses the gift to reassure them their disobedience would not cost them their lives. After the storm came as Paul foretold, his life became precious in the sight of the guards and they gave heed to his word. Remember, the gifts are grace gifts, not judgment gifts. When someone doesn't heed your warning, this is not a reason to judge them. It simply opens up another avenue of ministry for the grace of God.

The word of wisdom can also reveal itself as instructional when one is seeking direction and has no natural means of getting those instructions. The word of wisdom reveals the manifold wisdom of

God in situations where man's wisdom is not sufficient for the task at hand.

The word of wisdom was used this way as an integral part of Jesus' ministry.

> [2]And saith unto them, Go your way into the village over against you: and as soon as ye be entered into it, ye shall find a colt tied, whereon never man sat; loose him, and bring him. [3]And if any man say unto you, Why do ye this? say ye that the Lord hath need of him; and straightway he will send him hither. [4]And they went their way, and found the colt tied by the door without in a place where two ways met; and they loose him. Mark 11:2-4

This word of wisdom gave the disciples instruction and guidance in a situation where direction was needed. Not only does scripture highlight the manifestations of this gift, it also demonstrates the necessity of the gift. The gift is available to those who are humble enough to acknowledge their insufficiencies.

There was a need which could not be met by the wisdom of man. In this case, they could not have known there would be a colt in this exact location which had never been ridden. Even if they had seen it before, they could not have known the owners would allow them to use him with only the words "the Lord hath need of him".

The wisdom of God always knows where the provisions will be, and always gives access to those who need it. Through the word of wisdom, man is given access to this power to align himself with the wisdom of God. This is what James is alluding to when he says if any man lacks wisdom let him ask of God (James 1:5).

CHAPTER FIVE

The Word of Knowledge

Although the word of knowledge is similar in application to the word of wisdom, there are important distinctions. Whereas the word of wisdom gives wisdom concerning future events, the word of knowledge gives knowledge of past, present, and/or future events. The word of knowledge is like reading someone's spiritual résumé. Through this gift, you'll find you're given access to specific information which cannot be gained by any natural channels. Those who witness the gift in operation will know it can only come from God:

> [47]Jesus saw Nathanael coming to him, and saith of him, Behold an Israelite indeed, in whom is no guile! [48]Nathanael saith unto him, Whence knowest thou me? Jesus answered and said unto him, Before that Philip called thee, when thou wast under the fig tree, I saw thee. [49]Nathanael answered and saith unto him, Rabbi, thou art the Son of God; thou art the King of

Israel. John 1:47-49

When Jesus released this word of knowledge to Nathaniel, he was convinced Jesus was the son of God. Why was this word so impactful to him? When Jesus called him "an Israelite indeed in whom is no guile," he could have been flattered. But Nathaniel wanted to know if Jesus was just talking or if there was a reason Jesus felt this way.

Through the word of knowledge, Jesus proved He had information about Nathaniel's life He could not have known. First, Jesus knew his heart, which is why Jesus called him "one in whom there is no guile". Second, Jesus knew about his relationships. Jesus knew it was Phillip who called Nathaniel, and knew the location where he was called.

These things are also important for believers to know. Jesus knows your heart. He is familiar with your relationships. He knows where you are physically as well as spiritually. When Nathaniel realized Jesus had all this inside information, he realized it only could have come from God.

Another important aspect of this gift is the fact Jesus said He "saw" Nathaniel. This speaks of the administration, or operation, of the gift.

The word of knowledge not only gives you information, it can also bring comfort. In the book of Second Kings, there was a prophet by the name of Elisha. Elisha had a servant he was training with him. The servant became afraid because it looked like the enemy was about to overtake them. Elisha used the word of knowledge to bring his servant comfort.

> And he answered, Fear not: for they that be with us are more than they that be with them. And Elisha prayed, and said, LORD, I pray thee, open his eyes, that he may see. And the LORD opened the eyes of the young man; and he saw: and, behold, the mountain was full of horses and chariots of fire round about Elisha. II Kings 6:16-17.

Through the gift of the word of knowledge, Elisha helped his servant to be unafraid. This incident also showcases a key principle regarding the gifts of the spirit: the gifts are released in the lives of believers through prayer.

One of the greatest examples of the word of knowledge being released in the Bible can be found in the book of John:

> [16]Jesus saith unto her, Go, call thy husband, and come hither. [17]The woman answered and said, I have no husband. Jesus said unto her, Thou hast well said, I have no husband: [18]For thou hast had five husbands; and he whom thou now hast is not thy husband: in that saidst thou truly. John 4:16-18

Jesus, speaking to the woman at the well, releases a word of knowledge so powerful it penetrates her being and exposes the secrets of her heart. When it comes forth, it causes her to examine her life in a way which perhaps she never has before.

It is hard to resist the word when it is this powerful and probing.

She realized she could no longer pretend to be someone she was not. He exposed her lifestyle, relationship, and even gave her a history lesson on herself. In this case, the word of knowledge caused a complete turnaround in her life. It opened the door for further ministry which completely changes the course of her life.

The word of knowledge got her attention. At this point, Jesus was able to show her a need for the presence of the Holy Spirit in her life. This is evidenced by the fact she left her water pot and went into the city a transformed woman. As long as she had the water pot, she was trying to sustain herself on a temporary blessing, one which needed to be replenished every day. When she met Jesus, He replaced it with a river that would never run dry. The word was powerful, refreshing, and life changing.

It is important to understand when the word of knowledge is operating in the life of believers, it reveals knowledge in different ways. Sometimes you receive this information as impressions in your spirit. It can also be revealed audibly or visually in a dream or open vision.

The word of knowledge operates this way in the life of the prophet. This will be discussed in more detail when the office of the prophet is examined.

CHAPTER SIX

Discerning of Spirits

This gift of discerning of spirits can best be described as supernatural revelations of the spirits operating in and through individuals. Discerning of spirits gives you a unique view of the spiritual realm. Not only does this gift allow you to discern the spirits operating in individuals, it also allows you to bear witness of the Holy Spirit in operation.

Like the other gifts of revelation, discerning of spirits is a "seeing" gift. This is extremely important when spirits attempt to deceive you by offering counterfeits of the legitimate gifts operating through others.

You can see this gift fully in operation in the ministry of the Apostle Paul.

> [16]And it came to pass, as we went to prayer, a certain damsel possessed with a spirit of divination met us, which brought her masters much gain by soothsaying: [17]The same followed Paul and us, and cried, saying, These men are the servants of the most high God, which shew unto us the way of salvation. [18]And this did she many days. But Paul, being grieved, turned and said to the spirit, I command thee in the name of Jesus Christ to come out of her. And he came out the same hour. Acts 16:16-18

The scriptures tell us this woman was possessed with a spirit of divination. However, this is not evidenced by the words she uttered. When you examine what she was saying, it is evident she was speaking truth.

Think about it for a minute. Someone is doing the work of the ministry and trying to impact the town for Jesus. This woman shows up who is confirming everything they're doing and letting everyone know they're the real deal. This is free advertisement they didn't have to ask for. What could possibly be wrong with that?

This is why the gift of discerning of spirits is so important in ministry. Familiar spirits and other demonic forces can imitate spiritual gifts so well, one who is not familiar with the spiritual realm can be easily deceived. Not all spirits will manifest speaking words of blasphemy or otherwise making themselves easily recognizable. Spirits are too intelligent for this.

> And no marvel; for Satan himself is transformed into an angel of light. II Cor. 11:14

Sometimes it looks right and says all the right things, but

something tells you it is wrong. Remember, spiritual things are spiritually discerned.

This knowing goes beyond the five senses. Our five senses can be easily deceived. They are similar to the five foolish virgins. Our eyes are foolish enough to believe everything they see and our ears foolishly believe everything they hear. The gift of discerning of spirits allows us to see and hear beyond the ability of our eyes and ears.

Through this gift, Paul was able to discern what he was hearing was not of God, and he cast out the spirit trying to entice him through flattery. He was able to discern this spirit was trying to use his ministry to gain legitimacy in a movement which had come to displace it. Spirits are intelligent enough to recognize when something or someone is moving in on their territory. Recognizing Paul and Silas represented a force more powerful than itself, rather than lose all its influence, the spirit thought it could still maintain a degree of influence by endorsing the prevalent move of God. It's the same old trick: if you can't beat them, join them. Paul recognized the tactic and intent of the enemy and did not allow himself to be deceived.

This gift, like all gifts, was manifested in Jesus' ministry:

> 22Then Peter took him, and began to rebuke him, saying, Be it far from thee, Lord: this shall not be unto thee. 23But he turned, and said unto Peter, Get thee

> behind me, Satan: thou art an offence unto me: for thou savourest not the things that be of God, but those that be of men. Matt. 16:22-23

Again the enemy is attempting to use flattery to turn Jesus away from God's purposes. When he can't use you, he will find someone who is close to you. The enemy will leverage his attacks any way he can, but his goal is always the same. He wants to defeat you, whether by trickery, deceit, or any means necessary.

Not only did Jesus know the spirit's purpose, He also recognized the spirit trying to deceive him. This was no run of the mill demon or low ranking spirit. This was Satan himself. He was taking no chances with the son of God.

The scripture says Jesus turned to Peter, yet he addressed the spirit operating in Peter. Paul could've been deceived if he was seeking vainglory. Jesus could have been deceived if He was looking for an easy way out. This same gift is available to the church today if only the people of God desired spiritual gifts.

If you are to survive the attacks of the enemy, you must master singleness of purpose. You have to desire the things of God more than the things of the world. You must be filled with the Spirit and have the gifts operating in your ministry. Discerning of spirits allows you to recognize the enemy for who he is, regardless of how he shows up.

As in some of the other examples of this gift of the Spirit, when this gift is in operation, men and women are able to see things for what they really are. One of the key weapons Satan uses is deception, but through the gift of discerning of spirits, he is disarmed and the truth is known in situations the enemy would have used to promote a lie.

PART III:
Gifts of Power

> [4]And my speech and my preaching was not with enticing words of man's wisdom, but in demonstration of the Spirit and of power: [5]That your faith should not stand in the wisdom of men, but in the power of God. I Cor. 2:4-5

Through gifts of power, the power of God is made available to ordinary men. When Jesus returned to the Father, He knew the disciples' mission would be extremely hard. He knew they would come under fierce attacks of the enemy. They would need supernatural power to withstand the enemy's attacks and defeat him. This power couldn't come from man; it could only come from God. Therefore, Jesus gave His disciples specific instructions:

> And, behold, I send the promise of my Father upon you: but tarry ye in the city of Jerusalem, until ye be endued with power from on high. Lk. 24:49

The gifts of power are action gifts. They demonstrate the power of

God in unusual ways. With these gifts, men and women are empowered in the spiritual realms:

> For the kingdom of God is not in word, but in power.
> I Cor. 4:20

During the days of the apostles, the church was experiencing unprecedented growth and development. With this growth came new challenges. Sorcerers, witches, and wicked leaders saw their power base being challenged. They were not about to give up this territory without a fight. Through the gifts of power, the apostles were able to confront evil and establish the kingdom of God in the earth realm. The gifts in this category include miracles, healing, and faith.

CHAPTER SEVEN

Miracles

Miracles are events which cannot be explained by the laws of nature and are not the result of man's ability. Miracles occur when there are no natural means to meet a natural need. Miracles are evidence of the power of God demonstrated by His servants.

Many times in Jesus' ministry, miraculous events are recorded which defy human explanation. Some of the miracles Jesus performed were known as sign miracles. These miracles defied human explanation and demonstrated to man what was possible in the spiritual realm by reflecting it on earth.

The first recorded miracle of Jesus is turning water into wine. This is an example of a sign miracle. The water was turned into wine because there was a need. Although the need was urgent--a prerequisite for a miracle- this was also an excellent opportunity to demonstrate what was possible in the spirit.

In sign miracles, everything is impacted by the miracle and included in the sign. For instance, this miracle was done at a wedding. This is symbolic of Christ and the church. The water of the Holy Spirit represents the cleansing power of God to change lives and the wine represents the joy of the Lord. A close examination of this miracle affords you an opportunity to carefully review all the signs prevalent in it.

This miracle can be found in the second chapter of John verses 1-10:

> [1]And the third day there was a marriage in Cana of Galilee; and the mother of Jesus was there:

Notice the wedding was on the third day. This sign represents the power of the resurrection, as Jesus would be raised on the third day. Three is also the number of the trinity, or the triune nature of God.

> [2]And both Jesus was called, and his disciples, to the marriage. [3]And when they wanted wine, the mother of Jesus saith unto him, they have no wine. [4]Jesus saith unto her, Woman, what have I to do with thee? Mine hour is not yet come.

Jesus is invited to the wedding. This is symbolic of the Holy Spirit, because He will only come where He is invited.

Jesus' mother requests wine. Initially Jesus dismisses her request as if He will not grant it. Still, his mother gently places a demand on the anointing she knows is inside Him. She wasn't making a request to the son she bore, but to the God who was inside of Him. When you understand the woman is always symbolic of the church, you understand her ability to press past what appears to be a "no" to her request.

> [5]His mother saith unto the servants, Whatsoever he saith unto you, do *it*.

Now she places the weight of the request in Jesus' hands. It is no longer her responsibility, but His. Maybe this is the reason many don't receive their miracles. They lack the ability to put it in the hands of the only One who can do it.

> [6]And there were set there six waterpots of stone, after the manner of the purifying of the Jews, containing two or three firkins apiece.

This aspect of the miracle is very important, because it gets to the heart of the sign. There are six water pots. The number six is important because it is the number of man. Man without God is always limited. Until Jesus shows up, these will always be water pots. They will always contain water. Without Him, man will at most be ordinary.

> [7]Jesus saith unto them, Fill the waterpots with water. And they filled them up to the brim. [8]And he saith unto them, Draw out now, and bear unto the governor of the feast. And they bare it.

It is only when faith is mixed with ordinary the exceptional is created. As you witness the power of the miracle, what becomes evident is the servants were only told to put water in the vessels. This is easy enough to understand, because the vessels were designed to contain water and there was plenty of water available.

No faith is required for what is reasonable and acceptable.

Real faith shows up when you are asked to do the impossible. Pouring in did not require authentic faith, but drawing out did. When they were told to draw out, they were also instructed to give to the governor of the feast. This man, who was in charge of the feast, was not there to taste water. He was expecting to be given wine. When they poured it in, it was only water. When they drew it out, it could very well have still been only water. It wasn't required to be wine until it was delivered to the governor to taste.

The faith which fuels miracles only shows up when it is needed. This is what makes it so difficult for many people to walk in the miraculous. The faith used before the miracle is needed is wasted faith and seldom rewarded. This faith is only rewarded on an as needed basis.

The ten lepers in need of healing received their healing as they were in route. As in the physical realm, power is generated by motion. Miracles, like the other gifts of power, are activated by motion. The act of faith required to pour out water and serve it to the governor produced the power to transform water into wine. The gifts of faith and miracles work together and are almost inseparable.

> [9]When the ruler of the feast had tasted the water that was made wine, and knew not whence it was: (but the servants which drew the water knew;) the governor

of the feast called the bridegroom, ¹⁰And saith unto him, Every man at the beginning doth set forth good wine; and when men have well drunk, then that which is worse: but thou hast kept the good wine until now.

Notice what verse nine says. The governor did not know it was water, but the servants who drew the water knew. This is crucial, because it shows the transformation only took place when it was served to the governor. When the water was being drawn to be served, it was only water. This can generate enough fear in those who aren't mature to cause them to draw back. Even though faith is available to everyone, the faith to do miracles is not given to everyone.

Place yourself in those servants' position for a moment. You pour in water, and you draw out water, yet you are serving it to someone who is expecting to drink wine.

This fact brings to mind what the word says in Amos 3:7:

Surely the Lord God will do nothing, but he revealeth his secret unto his servants the prophets.

The servants knew the secret, that the water was turned into wine. Yet the governor who received the miracle didn't have a clue. His faith was not necessary. Many times when you see miracles in the Bible the person receiving the miracle is unaware the miracle is taking place. However the person who is performing or at least in on the miraculous is fully aware, and is responsible to give God the glory.

The words of the governor of the feast are also for a sign. He says every man always presents his best first. I hope you don't think he is only talking about wine. This is true in every area from work to relationships. You have probably heard the sentiment first impressions are the most lasting. Sometimes people invest so heavily in the first impression they have nothing better to offer after it.

The governor of the feast was expecting the quality of the wine to be inferior, but he was pleasantly surprised to find it to be superior. In fact, you can gather from his statement this experience was contrary to human nature as he understood it. This is a sign which shows when you trust God for the miraculous, He exceeds our expectations.

Another type of miracle is the miracle of provision. You can find an example of this miracle in the Old Testament:

> [4]So he went with them. And when they came to Jordan, they cut down wood. [5]But as one was felling a beam, the axe head fell into the water: and he cried, and said, Alas, master! for it was borrowed. [6]And the man of God said, Where fell it? And he shewed him the place. And he cut down a stick, and cast it in thither; and the iron did swim. [7]Therefore said he, Take it up to thee. And he put out his hand, and took it. II Kings 6:4-7

This need was one of urgent unanticipated need. If you only focus on the fact the metal rose up in the water when it should have sank, you miss the most important part of the miracle. Focusing only on the supernatural will also cause you to miss miracles which occur in your life every day.

This man had an urgent need he could not meet by ordinary means. The loss he was facing in his mind was catastrophic. If you have ever been in this type of situation and God moved for you, your miracle was just as real as his. Maybe God did not suspend the laws of nature, but maybe He allowed you to be released from prison after you had broken the laws of man, and suspended your sentence.

When you see them for what they truly are, you recognize you experience miracles on a regular basis. Not everyone will walk in the supernatural gift of miracles, but miracles are a part of everyday lives. When you acknowledge the everyday miracles, it increases your faith and prepares you for the supernatural gift of miracles.

CHAPTER EIGHT
Healing

Gifts of healing are divine interventions which bring wholeness, wellness and emotional, physical or spiritual healing. It is the only gift listed in the plural as gifts. This implies healing can be manifested through many avenues, including the hands of doctors who are led by the Holy Spirit.

Because man is a triune being, the need for healing can exist in three different realms: body, soul, and spirit. The triune nature of man is addressed by Paul in his letter to the Thessalonian church:

> And the very God of peace sanctify you wholly; and I pray God your whole spirit and soul and body be preserved blameless unto the coming of our Lord Jesus Christ. I Thess. 5:23

Spiritual Healing

Sometimes the people of God can get so involved in the mundane realm they forget they're spiritual beings first. Because people are spiritual beings, sometimes healing is needed as a result of illnesses stemming from spiritual conditions. These conditions can manifest in the body realm and cause sickness and disease.

In the fifth chapter of the book of Second Kings, the story of a leper named Namaan is related. When Namaan presents himself to the prophet to be healed, he is instructed to dip seven times in the Jordan River. By his response, it is obvious he is filled with pride. By dipping in the Jordan, he displays humility. This helps him resolve his pride issue and makes healing possible in his body as well.

There are also times when one can become wounded in their spirit. These wounds can be the result of assaults on your spirit from demonic forces bent on your destruction. The effects of these attacks can wreak havoc on the body as well as the spirit. Spiritual wounds left unchecked can lead to all sorts of physical symptoms which can plague a person throughout their life.

The Proverbial writer alludes to this fact when he wrote the following:

> The spirit of a man will sustain his infirmity; but a wounded spirit who can bear? Proverbs 18:14

The word sustain is derived from the Hebrew word "kuwl", which means to contain, or nourish. The word infirmity is derived from the Hebrew root word "machăleh", which means sickness or disease. The beginning of this scripture implies healing is first manifested in the spiritual realm. Therefore one whose spirit is strong is in a better position to fight off disease and sustain illness in the body.

The last portion of this scripture poses a question. Who can bear a wounded spirit? Even doctors concede patients in the hospital who are in good spirits have a better chance of recovery. Therefore, if you are going to discuss healing, you cannot ignore the spiritual realm.

When there is a need for healing in the spirit, it is usually because of spiritual bondage. Jesus encountered a woman who may have been dismissed as a woman with a bad back, but in the spirit He recognized something else was at play.

> [11]And, behold, there was a woman which had a spirit of infirmity eighteen years, and was bowed together, and could in no wise lift up herself. [12]And when Jesus saw her, he called her to him, and said unto her, Woman, thou art loosed from thine infirmity. [13]And he laid his hands on her: and immediately she was made straight, and glorified God. Lk. 13:11-13

In this case, you can see the gifts of the Spirit working in concert. Through discerning of spirits, Jesus recognized the woman's physical condition was a result of spiritual bondage. The healing she needed was spiritual. Medical doctors, without this spiritual knowledge and unaware of her need for deliverance, were unable to help her. After He dealt with her spiritual need, Jesus laid hands on her and she was able to receive physical healing.

Sometimes the spirit can be wounded as a result of sin, which can manifest itself throughout generations. This is what some people describe as generational curses operating in the bloodline. This may be what the disciples thought they were dealing with in the gospel of John.

> [1]And as Jesus passed by, he saw a man which was blind from his birth. [2]And his disciples asked him, saying, Master, who did sin, this man, or his parents, that he was born blind? John 9:1-2

As you read the scripture, you discover although they were doctrinally sound in their assumptions, they were wrong in their conclusion. There are specific times noted in scripture where sickness and disease is directly linked to sin. Their mistake was in assuming this was the case in this particular situation. This is why the gifts of healing are expressed in plurality.

> [5]When Jesus saw their faith, he said unto the sick of the palsy, Son, thy sins be forgiven thee. [6]But there was certain of the scribes sitting there, and reasoning in their hearts, [7]Why doth this man thus speak blasphemies? Who can forgive sins but God only? [8]And immediately when Jesus perceived in his spirit that they so reasoned within themselves, he said unto them, why reason ye these things in your hearts? [9]Whether is it easier to say to the sick of the palsy, Thy sins be forgiven thee; or to say, Arise, and take

up thy bed, and walk? Mark 2:5-9

In the above case, healing wasn't possible until the sin issue was dealt with. The scribes and Pharisees weren't able to deal with the sin issue; therefore, they weren't able to offer healing. Jesus, having the power to forgive sins, was able to bring healing to the whole man. Not every sickness is the result of sin, and Jesus did not deal with the sin issue every time he healed someone. If you are to deal with the spiritual realm, you must be led by the Holy Spirit.

Sickness and disease don't always originate in the spirit of man. Sickness can also manifest from the soulish realm. Healing in the soulish realm is needed when someone is broken or bruised as a result of emotional pain and trauma. This can be the result of betrayal, abuse, unprocessed pain, and unresolved issues.

The word "soul" is transliterated from the Greek word "psyche". Words like psychology are derived from "psyche". It literally means the seat of the feelings, desires, affections, aversions (our heart, soul etc.). (Strong's). The soul is where all of the feelings are stored. It is the seat of the emotions and affections.

The soul is similar in function to the software driving a computer. If you wanted to sabotage a computer, it wouldn't be necessary to alter the hardware if you had access to the software. By tampering with the software, you could affect the operation of the entire system. Just as the software of the computer can be accessed from a remote location, the same thing is possible with the soul.

The soul can be impacted by your relationships, experience, and most adversely by your pain. The soul is a virtual petri dish where the pain of past issues grows and compounds to affect all of your being. There is also a mind-body connection which is still not fully understood.

Through this connection, the emotional trauma you experience can also affect your physical well-being. For instance, it is a well-known fact most chronic conditions in the body are compounded by the level of stress a person is experiencing. This is surface level proof certain illnesses in the body and your physical well-being are connected to the condition of the soul.

[25]And a certain woman, which had an issue of blood twelve years, [26]And had suffered many things of many physicians, and had spent all that she had, and was nothing bettered, but rather grew worse, [27]When she had heard of Jesus, came in the press behind, and touched his garment. [28]For she said, If I may touch but his clothes, I shall be whole. [29]And straightway the fountain of her blood was dried up; and she felt in her body that she was healed of that plague. [30]And Jesus, immediately knowing in himself that virtue had gone out of him, turned him about in the press, and said, Who touched my clothes? [31]And his disciples said unto him, Thou seest the multitude thronging thee, and sayest thou, Who touched me? [32]And he looked round about to see her that had done this thing. [33]But the woman fearing and trembling, knowing what was done in her, came and fell down before him, and told him all the truth. [34]And he said unto her, Daughter,

thy faith hath made thee whole; go in peace, and be
whole of thy plague. Mark 5:25-34

There have been many sermons preached and books written which
have addressed this woman with the issue of blood. Yet how much
is really known about her condition? She had a condition connected
to an unrestrained flow of blood. The Bible only describes it as an
issue. This issue had impacted every area of her life. It is amazing
how issues, when they remain unresolved, can flow into other
areas of your life. By the time you meet this woman in scripture,
life had reduced her to a woman with an issue.

What began as a health issue grew to become a financial, hygiene,
social and religious issue. Nearly all these issues flow from the
soulish realm. In order for her to be healed, her healing had to be
initiated in the soulish realm. If it was merely a physical condition,
the physicians of her day should have been able to help her.
Instead, they only succeeded in taking all her money which led to
another issue-- financially depleting her resources. After twelve
horrendous years, there is probably no known remedy she wouldn't
have tried.

By the time she meets Jesus, she's beyond the need for physical
healing. Although she is seeking physical healing, He recognized a
deeper need in her. All the pain of the past had multiplied over the
years, leaving her feeling isolated and rejected. When she touched
his garment, the physical symptoms were gone, yet Jesus

recognized a deeper need.

When Jesus asked "who touched me?", it gave her an opportunity to express her emotional pain and find release from the torture she'd endured over the years, which had built up in her. At this point, Jesus was able to minister to the source of her sickness. Releasing her from the pain of her past, she was made whole. He gave her life back to her, and released her from the prison of her past.

Again, in this example, you can see the gifts working in concert in Jesus. You see the gift of healing along with the gift of faith operating in the woman with the issue of blood. Everyone is given a measure of faith, but it is important to recognize her faith initiated this encounter. In her spirit there was faith, but her soul was cluttered with fear and pain. This pain amplified a physical condition in her body which culminated into an issue that could not be resolved.

Unresolved issues and unprocessed pain plague many of the people of God. This is what the prophet Jeremiah was alluding to when he made this statement:

> Is there no balm in Gilead; is there no physician there?
> Why then is not the health of the daughter of my people recovered? Jer. 8:22

Jesus is the balm which brings healing not only to the body, but also to the soul. This is where the healing is needed most. This doesn't only apply to individuals. Sometimes the soul of a nation needs healing from the pain of the past.

Physical Healing

The body realm belongs to science and medicine. Conditions originating in this realm are usually easily treatable and in most cases will heal themselves if not affected by conditions in the soul and spirit. Most of the chronic conditions which afflict man are usually the result of spiritual or emotional bondage. The body becomes the stage where these conditions are acted out and manifest themselves.

This is not to belittle any physical condition. Any condition in the body left unchecked can lead to chronic suffering and death. When you discover the origin of diseases in the body realm, it allows you the insight needed to seek God for healing. Healing for all diseases was made available on the cross.

> But he was wounded for our transgressions, he was bruised for our iniquities: the chastisement of our peace was upon him; and with his stripes we are healed. Is. 53:5

Many Christians have read this scripture or at times have had it preached to them, but have you ever taken the time to research it fully and discover its deeper meaning? As you study the scripture in the original Hebrew, it sheds more light on what the scripture is conveying to the believer.

Wounded means to profane, defile, pollute, or desecrate. Transgression means rebellion against God. To transgress is to cut across or go against. It becomes easier to understand why someone who transgresses God's law would become wounded.

There are laws of nature which have severe consequences when you transgress them. You may not think of them as laws but they are just as consistent as all laws. For instance, if you stay away from fires, you won't get burnt. If you transgress this simple law, you will get burned and wounded.

The good news for believers is although you have transgressed God's laws, Jesus has taken the wounds. Most of the time when you think of wounds, you think of something easily healed and not of any real concern. Sometimes this is true, especially for surface wounds. But wounds left untreated can also lead to death. Sometimes cancer starts off as a wound that is never treated. As it grows and generates more cancerous cells, it can eventually lead to death. His wounds were for our wounds.

The scripture also says He was bruised. Bruised means to crush, be crushed, or become contrite. To be bruised indicates something more than a surface level wound. You can be wounded without leaving a bruise. Bruises tend to stay with you longer and represent a deeper hurt.

Notice also He was bruised for our iniquities. The word "iniquities" is a little more serious than transgression. Iniquities means perversity, depravity, guilt or punishment of iniquity. Iniquities are sins which are habitual and usually generational. They bruise not only the body but the spirit of man. When the disciples asked Jesus in the ninth chapter of John "who did sin that caused this man to be born blind", they were inferring iniquity as a result of perversion or depravity which is transmitted to the bloodline and manifests itself as generational curses.

When there is transgression and iniquity, the result is chastisement. Chastisement means discipline, chastening, or correction. When chastisement is offered, it is never pleasant. In fact, it tends to make you uncomfortable and denies you the ability to enjoy the fruit of transgression. It also takes away your peace.

Peace is defined as completeness, soundness, and welfare. All of this is taken away as a result of sin. This also leads to sickness and disease in the body. Disease can be described as a lack of peace. The word disease is derived from two words: "dis" which means against or contrary to, and "ease" which is peace or rest. A body which is diseased is one not at peace or rest.

A body without Jesus is at the mercy of sickness and disease. This body knows no peace, because it is through Him one has peace. He took the stripes you and I deserve so you can have the healing which belongs to Him.

Often when someone is sick, people quote the portion of this scripture which says "with his stripes we are healed". This is true, but have you ever thought about who takes the stripes when you're not saved, and what these stripes represent?

The word translated as "stripe" is also translated as bruise, wound, or blow. Scripture indicates there is a time for stripes:

> If they break my statutes, and keep not my commandments; Then will I visit their transgression with the rod, and their iniquity with stripes. Ps. 89:31-33

In this instance, stripes are the punishment for lawlessness. This doesn't explain how they can result in healing. To better understand this, you should look at another scripture.

> The blueness of a wound cleanseth away evil: so do stripes the inward parts of the belly. Prov. 20:30

This could be the connection many fail to make. Proverbs states "the blueness of a wound cleanseth away evil". Although the wound might be hurtful to our bodies, it minsters healing to our souls. Stripes do the same thing for the inward parts of the body.

This could have a twofold meaning. On one hand, inward parts could refer to the internal organs or unseen parts of the body. On the other hand, the word belly refers to the seat of hunger or, figuratively, the thing which drives you. It is conceivable one might believe if one receives stripes it could curtail certain behaviors. It could be seen as a cure for transgression.

Another thing which can affect your health more than some think is your attitude. There is no substitute for a healthy attitude. Your attitude is generally a reflection of your state of mind. When you find someone who constantly has a bad attitude or is easily upset, it is usually the result of bad or "stinking" thinking. Left unchecked, this could make it difficult for the person to receive healing even when it is available. According to the scriptures, your disposition can have a positive or negative effect on your health.

> A merry heart maketh a cheerful countenance: but by
> sorrow of the heart the spirit is broken. Prov. 15:13

When you allow negativity to get into your spirit and remain there until it effects your soul, the results can be devastating.

On the other hand, if you are able to maintain a healthy attitude even in the worst situations, it improves your outlook on life. In fact, a merry heart is described in Proverbs as medicine for the soul:

> A merry heart doeth good like a medicine: but a
> broken spirit drieth the bones. Prov. 17:22

By examining this scripture in the original Hebrew, it reveals an even deeper meaning in the lives of believers. The word "merry" is derived from a Hebrew word meaning joyful, merry, or glad. The emphasis here is on having a positive attitude which isn't merely a reflection of your present circumstances. It works just as well when things are not going your way.

The word heart is referring to the mind, will, heart, or understanding. In other words, it is referencing the soul. Your attitude is like the screensaver of your soul. It is a reflection of what's going on in your innermost being.

The word "broken" means to be stricken or wounded. Everyone experiences brokenness from time to time, but you have to find a way not to allow the brokenness to reach your spirit. This is why the scripture says to guard your heart.

Finally the word "drieth" in the original Hebrew means literally to make dry, wither, be dry, become dry, or be dried up. In other words, brokenness can drain the life from you and create conditions which fester all types of sickness and disease.

This same scripture gives the remedy. It reminds you to always keep a positive attitude despite your circumstances. No matter how your body is feeling, expect to get better. No matter what circumstances you're facing, expect them to change for the better.

CHAPTER NINE

Faith

Faith is described as a conviction of the truth of anything, belief; in the NT of a conviction or belief respecting man's relationship to God and divine things, generally with the included idea of trust and holy fervor born of faith and joined with it. Most people attempting to describe faith will default to Hebrews 11:1:

> Now faith is the substance of things hoped for, the evidence of things not seen.

This sounds good and preaches well, but there is much more to faith than this. This scripture was never intended to be a full definition of faith, but a springboard from which one could begin to describe the unfathomable power of faith.

Faith is the singularity from which all the gifts and fruits of the Spirit spring forth. It has the distinction of being the only gift of the spirit also listed among the fruit of the Spirit.

There are many examples in the Bible of faith moving men to perform exploits in the supernatural realm, but it also allows men to operate faithfully in the mundane realm. There are several benefits of faith listed in the eleventh chapter of the book of Hebrews.

> 2For by it the elders obtained a good report.

The same faith Jesus describes as moving mountains allowed the elders to obtain a good report. In other words, faith builds character. The importance of faith as a gift transcends the supernatural realm, and adds benefits to the natural realm.

Faith also enhances your understanding of the operation of the supernatural realm.

> 3Through faith we understand that the worlds were framed by the word of God, so that things which are seen were not made of things which do appear.

The things of the Spirit cannot be understood by natural means because they do not operate by natural understanding. There is no way to convince the natural man it is possible to walk on water. The very idea goes against everything one understands about the laws of nature. If you believe Jesus walked on water, you have to accept the fact the laws of nature were suspended to allow Him to do so. This simple act of belief requires faith uncommon to the natural man. The operation of faith and the understanding comes from the supernatural realm. It is given to the believer by faith.

> [4]By faith Abel offered unto God a more excellent sacrifice than Cain, by which he obtained witness that he was righteous, God testifying of his gifts: and by it he being dead yet speaketh.

According to verse four, faith has the ability to make our sacrifices acceptable unto God. Although there has been much speculation about why Abel's sacrifice was acceptable and Cain's was not, the writer of Hebrews lets the reader know the determining factor was faith. Sometimes it's not the amount you give, but the faith you exercise while giving which makes for a more excellent sacrifice. Although Abel was dead, his faith remained alive and spoke of more excellent things than the sacrifice of Cain.

Could it be the attitude Cain expressed while giving exposed the lack of faith he had in giving? One's attitude, which in the Old Testament is referred to as countenance, says more about one's faith than most people realize. This is especially true in regard to giving. Sacrifices not made willingly are not acceptable. When one is unwilling to give, it is reflected in one's disposition or countenance.

The apostle Paul reminds the believer the gift is not judged by the amount of money given as much as the amount of joy while giving:

> Every man according as he purposeth in his heart, so let him give; not grudgingly, or of necessity: for God loveth a cheerful giver. II Cor. 9:7

The gift of faith has the innate ability to transforms us.

> [5]By faith Enoch was translated that he should not see death; and was not found, because God had translated him: for before his translation he had this testimony, that he pleased God. Heb. 11:5

The translation of Enoch is one of the greatest miracles of faith recorded in the Bible. As he walked with God, he was transformed from flesh and blood into spirit. His faith is evident by the fact he pleased God.

It is important to remember pleasing God is not always the result of supernatural ability. In fact, supernatural ability is probably the least important to God. The faith expressed in excellent character is likely more pleasing to God.

Although the scriptures don't go into detail about what aspect of his life pleased God, faith was paramount in this statement. Hebrews 11:6 lets us know without faith it is impossible to please God.

Just as Enoch was transformed by faith, it takes faith to transform people from those whose sole desire is to please themselves into people who desire only to please God. Although Enoch's transformation was evident to all because he could not be found, your transformation is evident in the unseen realm. Even though people might still see you as the same person, they don't recognize your internal change. Unlike the butterfly, what is transformed in you can only be seen by faith.

Through your faith the invisible realm is made visible. No man has ever seen God with his natural eyes, yet by faith man believes God exists. The only way to see God is by faith.

What would you say if I were to tell you the only way God could see you was by faith? Faith allows God to see us, because it is the only thing which gets His attention. In the second chapter of the gospel of Mark, Jesus ministered in a house where the crowd grew so large there was no access through the door. Outside, four men, determined to get their friend before Jesus, tore off the roof and lowered their friend before Jesus. The Bible says when Jesus "saw" their faith, He ministered to their sick friend.

Although the house was crowded with people in need, the ones who got Jesus' attention were the ones whose faith could be seen.

Faith without works doesn't get God's attention because it can't be seen. Anybody can talk faith, but those who possess real faith put it into action. Noah's faith can be seen by his obedience to God. This is noted in verse seven:

> [7]By faith Noah, being warned of God of things not seen as yet, moved with fear, prepared an ark to the saving of his house; by the which he condemned the world, and became heir of the righteousness which is by faith.

He moved with fear because he believed what God said. This is the most important point to remember: faith which doesn't move you is not real faith. For instance, if someone gives you a tip in the stock market and you don't have faith in their information, you will not act on the tip. Conversely, if you had enjoyed success with their previous tips, you might be inspired to act on the information they provide to you.

Although faith allows you to be seen in the spiritual realm, when God wants to increase your faith, he chooses the ear gate.

> So then faith cometh by hearing, and hearing by the word of God. Rom. 10:17

It is not what you see, but what you hear which puts your faith into action and compels you to go forward. Jesus told the blind man to go and wash in the pool. He told the ten lepers to show themselves to the priest. These people acted in faith with no visible evidence beforehand. Walking by sight is not supposed to increase your faith. You don't wait until you see it to believe it. It is just the opposite: when you believe it, you will see it.

PART IV:
Auxiliary Gifts of the Spirit

Supernatural gifts of the Spirit are not all the Holy Spirit has to offer the believer. While these gifts are a blessing to the body and should be appreciated, there remain other gifts which are equally important and as much of a blessing to the body of Christ. These gifts are essential in the day to day operation of the church. They oftentimes go unnoticed and in many cases unrewarded.

Sometimes the desire to be used in the supernatural realm is the byproduct of our own vanity. This is why Paul said to covet earnestly the best gift. Since the Holy Spirit is the giver of the gift, it is His choice who moves in the supernatural and He knows not everybody is prepared for this realm. Just as He chose some to walk in healing and faith, there are others He chooses to use in the auxiliary gifts of the Spirit.

CHAPTER TEN
Helps

And God hath set some in the church, first apostles, secondarily prophets, thirdly teachers, after that miracles, then gifts of healings, helps, governments, diversities of tongues. 1 Cor. 12:28

One who operates in the gift of helps is one willing to give aid to the needy or serve in any area of the ministry where they can be of assistance. Those who have this gift are always seeking ways they can be of assistance to others. Someone blessed with the gift of helps will find themselves happiest when they're able to assist others in ministry.

This gift is not coveted by those who are vain and only desire to promote themselves. The gift of helps resides in those willing to stay in the background and allow others to shine. This does not mean your gift will go unnoticed or be without reward.

Jesus made himself of no reputation, yet His name is known and worshipped by all generations.

The best way to appreciate the gift of helps is to see it in operation in the Old and New Testament.

> 8And it fell on a day, that Elisha passed to Shunem, where was a great woman; and she constrained him to eat bread. And so it was, that as oft as he passed by, he turned in thither to eat bread. 9And she said unto her husband, Behold now, I perceive that this is an holy man of God, which passeth by us continually. 10Let us make a little chamber, I pray thee, on the wall; and let us set for him there a bed, and a table, and a stool, and a candlestick: and it shall be, when he cometh to us that he shall turn in thither. 11And it fell on a day, that he came thither, and he turned into the chamber, and lay there. II Kgs. 4:8-11

Many Old Testament students are familiar with the story of the Shunammite woman. She is an excellent example of someone used mightily in the gift of helps. This story brings to light many facets of the gift of helps.

First, this woman has been placed in the life of the man of God for a specific purpose. God never places you in a circumstance where He would use you in a way He has not already made provisions for you. Still, it must be understood even the provisions are in accordance to His purposes.

The Bible says she was a great woman. The word "great" is derived from the Hebrew word gadowl. Strong H1419. This word means someone of substantial means. She had the ability to do what God compelled her to do. Before you are called, the provision has already been made for your calling. People who are called to the ministry of helps are provided with the means to help in the capacity to which they are called.

Since this woman is married, it is important to note her husband is in agreement with her decision to help the man of God. When it comes to marriage, it is important Christians are not unequally yoked. This is especially true for those who are gifted with the ministry of helps. These people must feel free to utilize their gifting and unique calling in the body of Christ.

Her first instinct was to feed the man of God. Food is a basic need everyone has and she saw an opportunity to meet this need in the life of the prophet. After spending some time with him, she realized she could also provide shelter from the elements while he was traveling. In colloquial terms, she turned her home into a Motel 6 and left the light on for him. These were not things she was told to do; these were things she felt compelled to do.

When the Holy Spirit is in operation in the body of Christ, it becomes His business to ensure needs are being met in the body. It was obvious the prophet had a need, and the Holy Spirit revealed this need to someone who had the means and the desire to meet the need.

The gifts are not for us to use at our discretion; they are for the

Spirit to use at His discretion. Of course, the prophet was not the only one who had needs. The woman also had needs which had never been expressed. This is the key to the ministry of helps. Those called to this ministry rarely think of themselves, yet God always has them on His mind.

> 12And he said to Gehazi his servant, Call this Shunammite. And when he had called her, she stood before him. 13And he said unto him, Say now unto her, Behold, thou hast been careful for us with all this care; what is to be done for thee? wouldest thou be spoken for to the king, or to the captain of the host? And she answered, I dwell among mine own people. 14And he said, What then is to be done for her? And Gehazi answered, Verily she hath no child, and her husband is old. 15And he said, Call her. And when he had called her, she stood in the door. 16And he said, About this season, according to the time of life, thou shalt embrace a son. And she said, Nay, my lord, thou man of God, do not lie unto thine handmaid. 17And the woman conceived, and bare a son at that season that Elisha had said unto her, according to the time of life.
> II Kgs. 4:12-17

These verses make a powerful point: when God positions you to be a help to the man of God, He exposes your needs to those you serve so they can intercede on your behalf. You're not called into the ministry of helps to be lorded over and ordered around. You are there to help the man of God. At the same time, God opens their hearts to see your need.

Her selfless nature was revealed in the fact she never asked for anything for herself even when given the opportunity. This is the heart of a servant who is gifted with the ministry of helps. Everyone has needs which go unmet in different seasons in their life. The key to ministry is being able to operate in spite of those needs.

Many people have been rendered ineffective in ministry because they feel they cannot be effective until a specific need is met. The truth may be the opposite. You may feel you need a particular position or degree to be effective in ministry. While this might make you more effective, there are still things you can do as you pursue those things you have need of.

This woman had a need dear to her, but it seemed so far from reach she wouldn't even voice it. Sometimes the pain of being denied something for so long makes it easier to convince yourself it is no longer a desire. It was obvious her husband was much older than her and by this time she'd accepted the fact she would remain childless. She'd gotten to the point where she accepted her condition as hopeless. She resolved to forget about her personal needs and attend to the needs of others.

The room she was preparing for the prophet was probably one she'd had in mind for a child of her own. But now she was resigned to the fact this would never be a reality she would enjoy. The thing this woman did not realize is the Holy Spirit was using her compassion for the man of God to stir up maternal instincts in her. As she prepared room for the things he needed, God was preparing her heart to receive her greatest desire.

Another good example of the ministry of helps can be found in the New Testament in the ministry of Paul:

> [13]And on the sabbath we went out of the city by a river side, where prayer was wont to be made; and we sat down, and spake unto the women which resorted *thither*. [14]And a certain woman named Lydia, a seller of purple, of the city of Thyatira, which worshipped God, heard us: whose heart the Lord opened, that she attended unto the things which were spoken of Paul. [15]And when she was baptized, and her household, she besought us, saying, If ye have judged me to be faithful to the Lord, come into my house, and abide there. And she constrained us. Acts 16:13-15

The Apostle Paul's ministry encompassed a large part of the known world at this time. He went as he was led by the Holy Spirit. Being a man of great faith, he learned to depend on God for provisions as he traveled.

In any endeavor God leads you, there will always be someone whom God has already prepared to bless you on the journey. Paul had received a vision to go to Macedonia. He knew his help was needed in the ministry there. He made no provisions for himself, trusting the Lord to make hotel reservations and pay for them. When you use extreme faith, God always makes extreme provisions. This time, the provisions showed up in the form of a woman named Lydia.

When Paul shows up, he's not sure what his assignment will be. In his vision, he saw a man beckoning him to come to Macedonia; however, when he arrived, he encountered women having a prayer meeting at the riverside. Lydia was a wealthy woman who made a living as a merchant. Again, you see the provisions of God placed in the hands of a woman blessed with the gift of helps. At no point did Paul express to Lydia he had a need. Yet she was observant enough to recognize and minister to his needs.

As she ministered to his natural needs, he ministered to her spiritual needs. This is how the body is blessed so there is no lack.

CHAPTER ELEVEN

Giving

The person who is blessed with the gift of giving receives joy from giving. They seek out people to give to and ways to give. Their giving is not limited to money or material things. They also give of their resources and their talents. Since God is the author of all gifts, He will make it His business to see they have the resources to give.

> But this I say, He which soweth sparingly shall reap also sparingly; and he which soweth bountifully shall reap also bountifully. II Cor. 9:6

When you give into the kingdom of God, you are sowing into the kingdom of God. In the verse above, Paul points out one of the most important principles concerning sowing into the kingdom: how you reap is a function of how you sow.

Those who express themselves in the gift of giving are always seeking ways to be a blessing. Just as the farmer cannot expect to harvest more than he sows, the giver realizes his harvest will always be governed by the seed he sows.

Giving should be a reflection of purpose:

> [7]Every man according as he purposeth in his heart, so let him give; not grudgingly, or of necessity: for God loveth a cheerful giver.

The heart of a giver is reflected not only in the amount he gives but also in the manner in which he gives. A true giver realizes the joy which comes from giving. As long as your heart is right, you should never suffer from your giving.

> [8]And God is able to make all grace abound toward you; that ye, always having all sufficiency in all things, may abound to every good work.

Not only does God make provisions for your giving, he makes ways for you to prosper in your giving, as you can see in the following verses:

> [9](As it is written, He hath dispersed abroad; he hath given to the poor: his righteousness remaineth for ever. [10]Now he that ministereth seed to the sower both minister bread for your food, and multiply your seed sown, and increase the fruits of your righteousness;) [11]Being enriched in every thing to all bountifulness, which causeth through us thanksgiving to God.

In this discourse Paul reminds believers they can only gain from giving. This is important for the believer to realize, because only to the extent he learns this truth will he be able to truly prosper in the things of the kingdom. Paul goes on to emphasize the truth this gift is for the needs of the saints:

> [12]For the administration of this service not only supplieth the want of the saints, but is abundant also by many thanksgivings unto God; [13]While by the experiment of this ministration they glorify God for your professed subjection unto the gospel of Christ, and for your liberal distribution unto them, and unto all men.

The gift of giving, like all gifts, is for the body of Christ. Notice Paul encourages them not only to give but to pray for the saints. Finally, he encourages them to be thankful unto God:

> [14]And by their prayer for you, which long after you for the exceeding grace of God in you. [15]Thanks be unto God for his unspeakable gift.

As I stated earlier, the attitude with which you give is as important, if not more important, than the amount you give.

One of the biggest mistakes people can make when it comes to giving is thinking the amount they give determines the blessing they will receive. First of all, if you're giving only because you're looking to receive, your giving might be in vain. There are only two ways you can give: in faith or not in faith. When giving is not done in faith, the amount you give is irrelevant. As people of faith, all you do must be done in faith. This is especially true when it comes to giving.

The word of God says He loves a cheerful giver. Yet it is impossible to be a cheerful giver if you're not a willing giver. This is why it is important when you teach on giving to stress the point one must first be willing.

This is something you can teach; however, you cannot give the gift of giving to anyone. Some gifts are latent inside of an individual waiting to come out. The value of teaching is it can stir up and encourage those gifts. Yet if the gift is not inside the individual, or the will to use it is not present, then there is only so much you can do. The gift of giving cannot be expected to be manifested in everyone.

There are times when you see the corporate manifestation of a gift, and it is a beautiful thing to behold. This is especially true in the gift of giving. In today's church, it is hard to imagine a time when someone takes up an offering and so much is given, the people have to be told to stop giving. In fact, it is usually the opposite. It can be downright disheartening to see people begging for money which should be given willingly. The church has lost its way when it comes to concepts like giving.

There is one word which would make giving an easier concept to embrace by everyone. This word can make the difference in begging people to give more and restraining people from giving too much. This word is "willing". To truly understand this concept, you will need to examine it in action in the Old Testament.

> Take ye from among you an offering unto the LORD: whosoever is of a willing heart, let him bring it, an offering of the LORD; gold, and silver, and brass. Ex. 35:5

This is a time when there was a specific requirement placed on those they were to receive an offering from: whosoever is of a willing heart. If you're not careful, you can deceive yourself by believing the key to giving is having. Lots of people have plenty but give little. Conversely, there are those who have little and give all. The deception is in believing it is easier to give all when you have little. The truth is the less you have the more you need it.

When they were taking up an offering in Jesus's day there was a woman whose giving impressed Jesus more than everyone else, yet she gave less than everyone else.

> For all they did cast in of their abundance; but she of her want did cast in all that she had, even all her living. Mark 12:44

Nobody was pressuring her to give. Maybe no one even expected her to give because of her financial condition. As long as you allow your circumstances to dictate your giving, you will always be ruled by your circumstances. Those who have the gift of giving have found a way to liberate themselves from their circumstances.

Take another look at what happened in Moses day.

> 21And they came, every one whose heart stirred him up, and every one whom his spirit made willing, and they brought the LORD's offering to the work of the

tabernacle of the congregation, and for all his service, and for the holy garments. [22]And they came, both men and women, as many as were willing hearted, and brought bracelets, and earrings, and rings, and tablets, all jewels of gold: and every man that offered offered an offering of gold unto the LORD. Ex. 35:21-22.

The people acknowledged there was a need for the house of God, and they were willing to give to meet this need.

This is the heart of a giver. They look for opportunities to give. They don't need to be persuaded or coerced, because when they give they are operating in the gift of giving.

The gift of giving doesn't just consist of giving of your finances; it also consists of giving of your abilities and your time. Look at what happened as the people's hearts were stirred up to give:

[29]The children of Israel brought a willing offering unto the LORD, every man and woman, whose heart made them willing to bring for all manner of work, which the LORD had commanded to be made by the hand of Moses. [30]And Moses said unto the children of Israel, See, the LORD hath called by name Bezaleel the son of Uri, the son of Hur, of the tribe of Judah; [31]And he hath filled him with the spirit of God, in wisdom, in understanding, and in knowledge, and in all manner of workmanship; [32]And to devise curious works, to work in gold, and in silver, and in brass, [33]And in the cutting of stones, to set them, and in carving of wood, to make any manner of cunning work. [34]And he hath put in his heart that he may teach, both he, and Aholiab, the son of Ahisamach, of the tribe of Dan. [35]Them hath he filled with wisdom of heart, to work all manner of work, of the engraver, and of the cunning workman, and of the embroiderer, in blue, and in purple, in scarlet, and in fine linen, and of the

> weaver, even of them that do any work, and of those
> that devise cunning work. Ex. 35:29-35

Not only does the Spirit stir the people to give of their resources, but He stirs up the people to give of their abilities. It is also important to note God gave those who did the work of the ministry the ability to do the work. Giving is easier when you acknowledge God is the source of the gift. They were doing the work God gave them the wisdom and the knowledge to do.

This is a time when you can witness the full effect of the gift of giving. Everything needed is provided. There is no lack and everyone is giving of their time and resources willingly.

You may be wondering why this isn't seen in today's church. There is more than one answer to this question, but somewhere in the equation you will find the word "willing". When the people are willing, you don't have to beg, force or coerce.

> For if there be first a willing mind, it is accepted
> according to that a man hath, and not according to
> that he hath not. II Cor. 8:12

The key to their giving was the fact they were willing. It was no secret their wealth was delivered into their hands by the hand of God. They were preparing to leave Egypt with nothing for their two hundred years of labor for Pharaoh. God instructed them to borrow of the Egyptians. This He did knowing they wouldn't have to repay them. When they borrowed of the Egyptians, they received everything they would need to build the Tabernacle in the wilderness. When your heart is prepared to give, God will make sure your hands have something to give.

> [29]The children of Israel brought a willing offering unto the LORD, every man and woman, whose heart made them willing to bring for all manner of work, which the LORD had commanded to be made by the hand of Moses. Ex. 35:29

> [3]And they received of Moses all the offering, which the children of Israel had brought for the work of the service of the sanctuary, to make it withal. And they brought yet unto him free offerings every morning. [4]And all the wise men, that wrought all the work of the sanctuary, came every man from his work which they made; [5]And they spake unto Moses, saying, The people bring much more than enough for the service of the work, which the LORD commanded to make. [6]And Moses gave commandment, and they caused it to be proclaimed throughout the camp, saying, Let neither man nor woman make any more work for the offering of the sanctuary. So the people were restrained from bringing. [7]For the stuff they had was sufficient for all the work to make it, and too much. Ex. 36:3-7

This is possibly the only place in the Bible where the offering received was too much, and the people had to be told to stop giving.

One of the names for God is El Shaddai, literally "the God of more than enough". He would not be the God He is if He did not give you more than He requires for His purposes. It is the nature of God to provide more than enough. You could have been happy with enough stars to see at night, but He made the stars in abundance. He made more than enough fish to feed all generations who would cast a net into the sea. When you give in abundance, you reflect the nature of the God who created us in His own image.

When God chooses a king to lead his people, God chooses a man who is able to reflect God in his image and dealings with God's people. No king in the history of Israel did this better than David.

David not only demonstrated God's judgments and leadership, but he also gave generously to the house of the Lord. David desired to build the house of the Lord, but he was forbidden to because he had blood on his hands. Someone else might have refused to give to the house of God since they wouldn't be remembered as the man who built the Lord a house.

One of the greatest benefits of the gift of giving is the ability to impact the life of others by activating the gift in them. When you spend time in the presence of givers, it makes you want to give more. This is especially true when those in leadership share the gift of giving with their followers. When others see your example of giving, they are more likely to give more themselves.

Everything in the kingdom of God brings forth after its own kind. Leaders who are givers are more apt to have members of their flock who share this gift. As they see your example, you stir up the gift in them. King David is a perfect example of this concept in action.

[1]Furthermore David the king said unto all the

congregation, Solomon my son, whom alone God hath chosen, is yet young and tender, and the work is great: for the palace is not for man, but for the LORD God. [2]Now I have prepared with all my might for the house of my God the gold for things to be made of gold, and the silver for things of silver, and the brass for things of brass, the iron for things of iron, and wood for things of wood; onyx stones, and stones to be set, glistering stones, and of divers colours, and all manner of precious stones, and marble stones in abundance. [3]Moreover, because I have set my affection to the house of my God, I have of mine own proper good, of gold and silver, which I have given to the house of my God, over and above all that I have prepared for the holy house. [4]Even three thousand talents of gold, of the gold of Ophir, and seven thousand talents of refined silver, to overlay the walls of the houses withal: [5]The gold for things of gold, and the silver for things of silver, and for all manner of work to be made by the hands of artificers. And who then is willing to consecrate his service this day unto the LORD? [6]Then the chief of the fathers and princes of the tribes of Israel and the captains of thousands and of hundreds, with the rulers of the king's work, offered willingly, [7]And gave for the service of the house of God of gold five thousand talents and ten thousand drams, and of silver ten thousand talents, and of brass eighteen thousand talents, and one hundred thousand talents of iron. [8]And they with whom precious stones were found gave them to the treasure of the house of the LORD, by the hand of Jehiel the Gershonite. [9]Then the people rejoiced, for that they offered willingly, because with perfect heart they offered willingly to the LORD: and David the king also rejoiced with great joy. 1 Chr. 29:1-9

David's generosity impacted the people so much they too were encouraged to give. Some theologians estimate the value of David's gift to the temple to exceed one billion dollars in today's terms. This is in spite of the fact David was told he could not build the temple.

David's generosity is reflected in the generosity of the people. They gave willingly of all their substance. The Bible says the people rejoiced and gave willingly. It is amazing how every time people go over the top in their giving you find the same word: willing. This one word defines the heart of a giver more than anything else.

Beginning with the king, the leaders of the nation and all the people gave willingly to the work of the temple. This was a massive undertaking, and it would take all the resources at the people's disposal to accomplish such a feat. It took Solomon over forty six years to construct the temple of God. When he was ready to build, the way had already been prepared by his father. David had the vision and God used him to make provision. He chose Solomon to build the temple. This could not have been possible without the heart of a giver.

Those who have the gift of a giver will make provisions throughout the kingdom of God, most of which they will never get credit for. This is not the reason they do it. They do it because they cannot help themselves. If there is a need and they have the resources, they will automatically give what's needed. It is as though they know intrinsically this is the reason they have what they have. They have no reservations about using what God has provided.

There are times when the gift cannot be obtained by ordinary means. Although much is left at your disposal, sometimes giving must be expressed sacrificially. When the occasion demands it, you can't give in a business as usual manner. On one of the darkest days in David's kingdom he found himself in need of a sacrifice. David had sinned by numbering the people of God against the advice of his counsel. When he realized he had sinned, David wanted to make a sacrifice offering to atone for his deeds.

This was a serious situation with David. Unlike the time when he had sinned with Bathsheba, this sin involved kingdom business. He knew if he was to seek forgiveness, he had to approach God correctly.

> [22]Then David said to Ornan, Grant me the place of this threshingfloor, that I may build an altar therein unto the LORD: thou shalt grant it me for the full price: that the plague may be stayed from the people. [23]And Ornan said unto David, Take it to thee, and let my lord the king do that which is good in his eyes: lo, I give thee the oxen also for burnt offerings, and the threshing instruments for wood, and the wheat for the meat offering; I give it all. [24]And king David said to Ornan, Nay; but I will verily buy it for the full price: for I will not take that which is thine for the LORD, nor offer burnt offerings without cost. [25]So David gave to Ornan for the place six hundred shekels of gold by weight. I Chr. 21:22-25

David was the king, and he was entitled to anything in the kingdom he desired. It would have been easy, and lawful, for him to accept the threshing floor offered to him by Ornan. No one would have questioned his actions and Ornan would have been honored to provide what the king needed at this time.

What David does in this instance helps explain why God called

David a man after His own heart. It was not Ornan who had sinned; it was David. Why should Ornan pay the price for David's sin? It was David who disobeyed God and allowed Satan to fill his heart with pride, and David felt he should pay.

David understood this was no ordinary gift. This was a sacrifice offering. He also understood a fundamental truth about sacrifice offerings: they cannot be made without cost. Sacrifice means I am offering beyond the value to me. In most cases sacrifices hurt because the price is often more than you feel you can afford at the time.

The threshing floor was offered to David for free, yet he gave a value he determined, which was more than fair market value. Acknowledging the seriousness of the situation, David didn't want to take his sacrifice lightly. He wanted it to feel like a sacrifice. He wanted it to cost him something significant.

The sacrifice Jesus made for us was not cheap. It was not something you could buy with corruptible silver and gold. It cost Him something He could feel. He paid the ultimate price for our redemption so no one could say He made a sacrifice which cost Him nothing. He didn't do this because of His sin. He did it for the sins of the world. Nothing about what He did was cheap. It came at a great price. Aren't you glad He was willing to pay the price?

CHAPTER TWELVE

Governments

The word "governments" is transliterated from the Greek word "kybernēsis", which is of Latin origin. It means "to pilot or steer, or church directorship". A more modern translation for the gift of governments is administration. In this book, the words are used interchangeably because they essentially have the same meaning.

The gift of governments has proven to be one of the most effective in establishing and maintaining the church as a business entity. This gift is reserved for those who would operate in church administration. They are given the awesome responsibility of providing direction for the church.

This gift is reserved for those who operate in church administration. The person who has this gift is responsible for setting the direction of the organization. They must also take responsibility for choices made which may or may not work out as planned.

In order for an organization to thrive in modern society, there has to be someone in charge. Christ is ultimately responsible for governing the body; yet men and women have been put in place by the Spirit with abilities to administrate the growth and direction of the church.

The gift of administration is a hybrid gift. Although listed as an auxiliary gift, it is closely linked to the ministry gifts discussed later. The gift of administration is not a five-fold ministry gift; however, anyone effective in the five-fold ministry will either be blessed with this gift, or have someone closely connected with them who possesses it. Lasting church growth is almost impossible without it.

Moses is one of the greatest examples in the Bible of how this gift is manifested. The gift of administration is used to preserve Moses's ministry at a time when he's feeling overwhelmed with the burden of leadership. As you examine these scriptures, you will find there is a lot to be learned from Moses' example as well as others in today's church:

> 13And it came to pass on the morrow, that Moses sat to judge the people: and the people stood by Moses from the morning unto the evening. 14And when Moses' father in law saw all that he did to the people, he said, What is this thing that thou doest to the people? why sittest thou thyself alone, and all the people stand by thee from morning unto even? 15And

Moses said unto his father in law, Because the people come unto me to enquire of God: [16]When they have a matter, they come unto me; and I judge between one and another, and I do make them know the statutes of God, and his laws. [17]And Moses' father in law said unto him, The thing that thou doest is not good. [18]Thou wilt surely wear away, both thou, and this people that is with thee: for this thing is too heavy for thee; thou art not able to perform it thyself alone. [19]Hearken now unto my voice, I will give thee counsel, and God shall be with thee: Be thou for the people to Godward, that thou mayest bring the causes unto God: [20]And thou shalt teach them ordinances and laws, and shalt shew them the way wherein they must walk, and the work that they must do. [21]Moreover thou shalt provide out of all the people able men, such as fear God, men of truth, hating covetousness; and place such over them, to be rulers of thousands, and rulers of hundreds, rulers of fifties, and rulers of tens: [22]And let them judge the people at all seasons: and it shall be, that every great matter they shall bring unto thee, but every small matter they shall judge: so shall it be easier for thyself, and they shall bear the burden with thee. [23]If thou shalt do this thing, and God command thee so, then thou shalt be able to endure, and all this people shall also go to their place in peace. [24]So Moses hearkened to the voice of his father in law, and did all that he had said. Exodus 18:13-24

Moses's ministry was compared to Jesus' more than anyone else in the Bible. They share more similarities than any other figures in the Bible. There is no doubt Moses was anointed and called of God. He was God's chosen vessel to lead the children of Israel out of Egypt. With all Moses had going for him, he still found himself being overwhelmed by leadership. The demands of leading so many people and trying to do it all alone were beginning to wear him out. Everyone in leadership must be aware of this danger, or they run the risk of finding themselves in the same position as Moses.

Moses' ministry was saved by an unlikely figure. Little information is given about Jethro in scripture. Scripture tells you Jethro was Moses's father-n-law and a priest of Midian. However, when you read the advice he gives to Moses, you discover Jethro was operating in the gift of governments.

The ability to delegate authority is far better than simply exercising authority. When you can appoint others to carry out the policies and procedures in place, then you are free to do other things pertinent to the position you're in. Jethro realized Moses' time could be better spent doing other things besides judging every matter brought before him. Those possessing the gift of governments have the ability both to see the problem and offer a solution.

Before anything could be delegated, there had to be rules in place everyone was aware of and understood. Moses' job initially was to ensure there were guidelines for the people to adhere to. Next, he had the task of making sure the leadership he placed in positions of authority understood and followed those rules. Once these concepts were established, it was the responsibility of the people he put in place to enforce the principles and guidelines he instituted.

What Jethro illustrated to Moses was the equivalent of the organizational chart used by most businesses today. Moses was at the top, like a president or administrator. Next came those who represented top management positions. These were the individuals who would be captains over thousands. After those were the ones equivalent to mid-level management. They were appointed over one hundred or fifty. Finally, the line supervisors who were captain over ten.

By using the structure Jethro outlined, Moses was able free up time he could spend with his family and with God. Too many ministers are burning themselves out because they are not using the resources God provided to the ministry. Those who either have the gift of governments or are surrounded by those who do will find themselves in a better position to lead God's people.

PART V

Ministry Gifts

> ⁸Wherefore he saith, When he ascended up on high, he led captivity captive, and gave gifts unto men… ¹¹And he gave some, apostles; and some, prophets; and some, evangelists; and some, pastors and teachers; Eph. 4:8, 11

Thus far, this book has examined many aspects of the gifts of the Spirit and how they are manifested in the lives of believers. The remainder of this book will focus on a unique set of gifts known as the fivefold ministry. These gifts were given to those called to do special work in the kingdom of God. Each office represents a unique calling and anointing.

As you examine the men in the Old and New Testament who walked in these offices, you will begin to understand the characteristics of these gifts unique to the office they were provided for.

These gifts serve a unique purpose:

For the perfecting of the saints, for the work of the ministry, for the edifying of the body of Christ. Eph. 4:12

CHAPTER THIRTEEN
Apostle

The word apostle comes from the Greek word Apostolos, which means "messenger or sent ones". Most of the time when the term "apostle" is used in the Bible, it is in reference to the twelve who were with Jesus. However, the Bible makes mention of several others who were not among the twelve, among them Barnabas, Silvanus, and perhaps the most famous of all, the apostle Paul.

There is not much known about the office of the apostle in today's church. Most of this is due to ignorance about the office, which has left some to conclude the office is no longer needed in today's church. Most of the confusion in regards to the office of the Apostle is derived from man's interpretation of the following passage of scripture:

> [15]And in those days Peter stood up in the midst of the disciples, and said, (the number of names together

were about an hundred and twenty,) [16]Men and brethren, this scripture must needs have been fulfilled, which the Holy Ghost by the mouth of David spake before concerning Judas, which was guide to them that took Jesus. [17]For he was numbered with us, and had obtained part of this ministry. [18]Now this man purchased a field with the reward of iniquity; and falling headlong, he burst asunder in the midst, and all his bowels gushed out. [19]And it was known unto all the dwellers at Jerusalem; insomuch as that field is called in their proper tongue, Aceldama, that is to say, The field of blood. [20]For it is written in the book of Psalms, Let his habitation be desolate, and let no man dwell therein: and his bishoprick let another take. [21]Wherefore of these men which have companied with us all the time that the Lord Jesus went in and out among us, [22]Beginning from the baptism of John, unto that same day that he was taken up from us, must one be ordained to be a witness with us of his resurrection. Acts 1:15-22

The death of Jesus left the apostles in dire straits. They were feeling betrayed by one of their own, and they felt abandoned. Although they had instructions to "tarry in Jerusalem", there were no further instructions given. They began to examine themselves, and ask hard questions. It is at this time they realize Judas' death left a vacancy in their ministry. They felt this position had to be filled in order to fulfill their mission.

In the verses above you find the apostles trying to define the qualifications of an apostle. There were no instructions given and no blueprints for them to follow. Without Jesus to guide them, they concluded the only qualification for an apostle was time spent with Jesus during his earthly ministry. This could help explain the belief the office of the apostle no longer exist in today's church.

Although on the surface this might seem like good judgment, and it allows them to continue on with their mission, this conclusion left gaping holes. There would be others used in the office of the apostle who were not a part of their ministry. If this means they were not real apostles then it leaves an even bigger hole. It brings into question the apostleship of perhaps the greatest apostle of all time.

The apostle Paul never spent time with Jesus during his earthly ministry. Yet he went on to write over two thirds of the New Testament, along with being responsible for the inclusion of the gentile believers.

The ministry of the apostle Paul is one followed by signs and wonders.

> Truly the signs of an apostle were wrought among you in all patience, in signs, and wonders, and mighty deeds. II Cor. 12:12

When God established the office of the apostle, it was confirmed by a demonstration of power and apostolic authority:

> [13]Now when they saw the boldness of Peter and John, and perceived that they were unlearned and ignorant men, they marvelled; and they took knowledge of them, that they had been with Jesus. [14]And beholding the man which was healed standing with them, they could say nothing against it. Acts 4:13-14

There was nothing about the appearances of John and Peter to show they were anything special, but the demonstration of power made their audience realize they had spent time with Jesus. This was the single requirement given for the office of an apostle. Anyone could say they had been with Jesus, but only those who truly had could demonstrate it with power.

This power was especially evident when it came to spiritual confrontations, and being filled with the Holy Spirit:

> 5Then Philip went down to the city of Samaria, and preached Christ unto them. 6And the people with one accord gave heed unto those things which Philip spake, hearing and seeing the miracles which he did. 7For unclean spirits, crying with loud voice, came out of many that were possessed with them: and many taken with palsies, and that were lame, were healed. 8And there was great joy in that city. 9But there was a certain man, called Simon, which beforetime in the same city used sorcery, and bewitched the people of Samaria, giving out that himself was some great one: 10To whom they all gave heed, from the least to the greatest, saying, This man is the great power of God. 11And to him they had regard, because that of long time he had bewitched them with sorceries. 12But when they believed Philip preaching the things concerning the kingdom of God, and the name of Jesus Christ, they were baptized, both men and women. 13Then Simon himself believed also: and when he was baptized, he continued with Philip, and wondered, beholding the miracles and signs which were done. Acts 8:5-13

The preaching of Phillip was dynamic and engaging. Although Phillip was being used mightily of God, he was not an apostle. Still he was able to get the people excited about the kingdom of God and usher them into salvation. As powerful as he was, he was limited in spiritual authority. When the people were ready to be filled with the Holy Ghost they had to call in the apostles:

> ¹⁴Now when the apostles which were at Jerusalem heard that Samaria had received the word of God, they sent unto them Peter and John: ¹⁵Who, when they were come down, prayed for them, that they might receive the Holy Ghost: ¹⁶(For as yet he was fallen upon none of them: only they were baptized in the name of the Lord Jesus.) ¹⁷Then laid they their hands on them, and they received the Holy Ghost. v 14-17

The apostles were not only there for the impartation of the Holy Spirit. God knew there would be a confrontation with evil. Simon had been in power for a long time and was not about to let go of his authority without a fight. Although Phillip was a powerful preacher, this battle would call for someone with apostolic power to confront the evil Simon the sorcerer represented.

> ¹⁸And when Simon saw that through laying on of the apostles' hands the Holy Ghost was given, he offered them money, ¹⁹Saying, Give me also this power, that on whomsoever I lay hands, he may receive the Holy Ghost. ²⁰But Peter said unto him, Thy money perish with thee, because thou hast thought that the gift of God may be purchased with money. ²¹Thou hast neither part nor lot in this matter: for thy heart is not right in the sight of God. ²²Repent therefore of this thy wickedness, and pray God, if perhaps the thought of thine heart may be forgiven thee. ²³For I perceive that thou art in the gall of bitterness, and in the bond of iniquity. ²⁴Then answered Simon, and said, Pray ye to the LORD for me, that none of these things which ye have spoken come upon me. ²⁵And they, when they had testified and preached the word of the Lord, returned to Jerusalem, and preached the gospel in many villages of the Samaritans. v 18-25

Simon saw something in Peter and John he did not see in Phillip.

They had the same Holy Ghost and were preaching the same message, but Simon saw John and Peter were walking in apostolic authority. He offered them money because he wanted the same authority they had.

Those who walk in apostolic authority exercise power over regions. They engage the powers in the atmosphere in those regions. Simon soon realized his money and witchcraft were no match for the anointing on their lives. In today's church, it is imperative for saints to realize what they have from God is not for sale, and can't be bought.

Apostleship of Paul

Paul's conversion is one of the most fascinating stories in the Bible. As you review the following scriptures, I want you to focus on the great lengths to which Jesus went to recruit Paul into the ministry of which Paul was the chief opponent.

> [1]And Saul, yet breathing out threatenings and slaughter against the disciples of the Lord, went unto the high priest, [2]And desired of him letters to Damascus to the synagogues, that if he found any of this way, whether they were men or women, he might bring them bound unto Jerusalem. [3]And as he journeyed, he came near Damascus: and suddenly there shined round about him a light from heaven: [4]And he fell to the earth, and heard a voice saying unto him, Saul, Saul, why persecutest thou me? [5]And he said, Who art thou, Lord? And the Lord said, I am Jesus whom thou persecutest: it is hard for thee to kick against the pricks. [6]And he trembling and astonished said, Lord, what wilt thou have me to do? And the Lord said unto him, Arise, and go into the city, and it shall be told thee what thou must do. [7]And the men which journeyed with him stood speechless, hearing a voice, but seeing no man. [8]And Saul arose from the earth; and when his eyes were opened, he saw no man: but they led him by the hand, and brought him into Damascus. Acts 9:1-8

There have been many sermons preached and books written on Paul's conversion experience. Most theologians agree Paul is perhaps one of the most prolific apostles in the early church. Unlike the other apostles, he was not a part of Jesus' earthly ministry. Yet he was without doubt used more than any other apostle, especially in outreach to the gentile believers.

When you consider the ways of God, they are considerably different than the ways of man. The disciples believed Judas could only be replaced by someone who had been with them the entire time of Jesus' earthly ministry. So when they chose a replacement they never thought to look beyond their own understanding. Yet when they chose a replacement for Judas, it was someone you never hear from again. What if this was not who God had in mind? What if the best person to replace a disciple who was with them and betrayed them was someone who was against them and joined them? If this was the case, then Paul would be the ideal replacement for Judas.

Before his conversion Paul succeeded in making quite a name for himself among those of the Jewish faith who opposed the Christian movement. Paul described himself as proud of his Jewish heritage:

> 5Circumcised the eighth day, of the stock of Israel, of the tribe of Benjamin, an Hebrew of the Hebrews; as touching the law, a Pharisee; 6Concerning zeal, persecuting the church; touching the righteousness which is in the law, blameless. 7But what things were gain to me, those I counted loss for Christ. Phil. 3:5-7

As you can see, Paul had all the right credentials, and was an up and coming leader in the Jewish faith. Yet when he encountered Christ, he was willing to give it all away.

Because Paul had not been with the original twelve, his apostleship would always be brought into question. He acknowledges this fact in his own writings.

> Paul, an apostle, (not of men, neither by man, but by Jesus Christ, and God the Father, who raised him from the dead;). Gal. 1:1

He openly acknowledges man did not certify his apostleship, nor did it conform to the timeline established by the apostles:

> [8]And last of all he was seen of me also, as of one born out of due time. [9]For I am the least of the apostles, that am not meet to be called an apostle, because I persecuted the church of God. I Cor. 15:8-9

Still, this does not change the fact he was God's chosen vessel.

> [9]And he was three days without sight, and neither did eat nor drink. [10]And there was a certain disciple at Damascus, named Ananias; and to him said the Lord in a vision, Ananias. And he said, Behold, I am here, Lord. [11]And the Lord said unto him, Arise, and go into the street which is called Straight, and enquire in the house of Judas for one called Saul, of Tarsus: for, behold, he prayeth, [12]And hath seen in a vision a man named Ananias coming in, and putting his hand on him, that he might receive his sight. [13]Then Ananias answered, Lord, I have heard by many of this man, how much evil he hath done to thy saints at Jerusalem: [14]And here he hath authority from the chief priests to bind all that call on thy name. [15]But the Lord said unto him, Go thy way: for he is a chosen vessel unto me, to bear my name before the Gentiles, and kings, and the children of Israel: [16]For I will shew him how great things he must suffer for my name's sake. Acts 9:9-16

Even Ananias was reluctant to minister unto Paul because of his reputation. Nothing about his life before his conversion would lead you to think he was chosen of God for salvation, let alone to be an apostle. This would be a test of Ananias' faith, for Ananias knew full well he was risking his life by reaching out to Paul. Yet he had no choice if he were to be obedient to Christ:

> [17]And Ananias went his way, and entered into the house; and putting his hands on him said, Brother Saul, the Lord, even Jesus, that appeared unto thee in the way as thou camest, hath sent me, that thou mightest receive thy sight, and be filled with the Holy Ghost. [18]And immediately there fell from his eyes as it had been scales: and he received sight forthwith, and arose, and was baptized. (v. 17-18)

This act of faith began the ministry of Paul, who was called Saul at the time.

> [19]And when he had received meat, he was strengthened. Then was Saul certain days with the disciples which were at Damascus. [20]And straightway he preached Christ in the synagogues, that he is the Son of God. (v. 19-20)

Although Paul would go on to become one of the greatest apostles of all time, his ministry would always be wrought with controversy.

> [21]But all that heard him were amazed, and said; Is not this he that destroyed them which called on this name in Jerusalem, and came hither for that intent, that he might bring them bound unto the chief priests? [22]But Saul increased the more in strength, and confounded the Jews which dwelt at Damascus, proving that this is very Christ. (v. 21-22)

As powerful and anointed as Paul was, he still struggled with the assumption he was not an apostle, because he did not spend time with Jesus during his earthly ministry. The grace of God is so amazing at times. Even though he did not spend time with Jesus during his earthly ministry, he still fulfilled the requirement in the spirit:

> [11]But I certify you, brethren, that the gospel which was preached of me is not after man. [12]For I neither received it of man, neither was I taught it, but by the revelation of Jesus Christ. [13]For ye have heard of my conversation in time past in the Jews' religion, how that beyond measure I persecuted the church of God, and wasted it: [14]And profited in the Jews' religion above many my equals in mine own nation, being more exceedingly zealous of the traditions of my fathers. [15]But when it pleased God, who separated me from my mother's womb, and called me by his grace, [16]To reveal his Son in me, that I might preach him among the heathen; immediately I conferred not with flesh and blood: [17]Neither went I up to Jerusalem to them which were apostles before me; but I went into Arabia, and returned again unto Damascus. [18]Then after three years I went up to Jerusalem to see Peter, and abode with him fifteen days. Gal. 1:11-18

Paul didn't spend time with Jesus during his earthly ministry, but he spent time with Him in the spirit. After his conversion, Paul didn't seek to be confirmed by man. Just as the disciples were taught by Jesus for three years, Paul was taught by the Holy Ghost for three years. After spending time with Jesus in the Spirit, he was qualified to be an apostle. His apostleship never had to be approved or confirmed by man because it originated in the mind of Christ.

CHAPTER FOURTEEN
Prophet

> And he said, Hear now my words: If there be a prophet among you, I the LORD will make myself known unto him in a vision, and will speak unto him in a dream. Num. 12:6

The office of the prophet is perhaps the most written about in scripture. Those who walked in this office were held in high regard by kings and others in power. Prophets were often sought for spiritual advice and counsel. Although there is much written about the office of the prophet, little is understood about this office, or its place in today's church.

The word prophet is derived from the Hebrew word (nabiy'), - who as actuated by a divine afflatus, or spirit, either rebuked the conduct of kings and nations, or predicted future events. (Hebrew Chaldee Lexicon).

The prophets were most known for their ability to "see" in the spiritual realm. Perhaps the most renowned of the Old Testament prophets is the prophet Samuel. He is the first judge of the nation of Israel who is also a prophet. God used him to lead and direct the nation when there was no king, and when the people desired a king, God chose a king for him to anoint as captain over the people:

> [2]When thou art departed from me today, then thou shalt find two men by Rachel's sepulchre in the border of Benjamin at Zelzah; and they will say unto thee, The asses which thou wentest to seek are found: and, lo, thy father hath left the care of the asses, and sorroweth for you, saying, What shall I do for my son? [3]Then shalt thou go on forward from thence, and thou shalt come to the plain of Tabor, and there shall meet thee three men going up to God to Bethel, one carrying three kids, and another carrying three loaves of bread, and another carrying a bottle of wine: [4]And they will salute thee, and give thee two loaves of bread; which thou shalt receive of their hands. [5]After that thou shalt come to the hill of God, where is the garrison of the Philistines: and it shall come to pass, when thou art come thither to the city, that thou shalt meet a company of prophets coming down from the high place with a psaltery, and a tabret, and a pipe, and a harp, before them; and they shall prophesy: [6]And the Spirit of the LORD will come upon thee, and thou shalt prophesy with them, and shalt be turned into another man. I Sam. 10:2-6

From these verses of scripture it is easy to ascertain why Samuel is called a seer. First, Samuel lets Saul know the most pressing thing on his mind has been taken care of. It is amazing how when one is exposed to the prophetic, he gains prophetic insight into seemingly unrelated events. It is evident Saul needed to see Samuel, but not for the reason he believed. Saul's primary reason for having to see Samuel is so Samuel can anoint him king of Israel.

He gives instructions to Saul as though he had walked the entire journey before him. This is not guessing, or relying on getting a certain percentage of the information to be correct. Notice the clarity of his instructions. Not only is he able to tell Saul who he will see, but what they shall do and what he is to do in response.

God is very precise in the words He speaks by the mouth of the prophet. This is how one is able to discern a true prophet of God from charlatans who speak out of their own mind:

> 21And if thou say in thine heart, How shall we know the word which the LORD hath not spoken? 22When a prophet speaketh in the name of the LORD, if the thing follow not, nor come to pass, that is the thing which the LORD hath not spoken, but the prophet hath spoken it presumptuously: thou shalt not be afraid of him. Deut. 18:21-22

As he is giving instructions to Saul, a very important truth about the prophetic emerges. He tells him he shall encounter a company of prophets. Then he tells him the Spirit of the Lord shall come upon him while he is in their presence. This is important because you see the impartation of the gift given to someone in close association to those who are walking in the office. This helps you to realize an important truth: when you are in the presence of the anointing, there is an overflow of the gift in the atmosphere.

While being in the company of the prophets, the prophetic gift began to overflow into the life of Saul, who was not a prophet. It is not unusual for people who are in an atmosphere charged by the anointing to operate in the same anointing. This does not make one a prophet, but his life has been impacted by the atmosphere he has been exposed to, and he finds himself prophesying.

The prophetic ministry emerged as a cushion between the people and God. In the book of Exodus, it became evident the people were afraid of God, and did not want to bear the responsibility of living a holy life. So they pleaded with Moses to be an intermediary, to stand in the gap for them. This established Moses as the first to hold the office of the prophet in the nation of Israel.

Although he was not the first prophet, he was the first to walk in an official capacity as the prophet and judge for the children of Israel before they became a nation with their own land:

> 14For these nations, which thou shalt possess, hearkened unto observers of times, and unto diviners: but as for thee, the LORD thy God hath not suffered thee so to do. 15The LORD thy God will raise up unto thee a Prophet from the midst of thee, of thy brethren, like unto me; unto him ye shall hearken; 16According to all that thou desiredst of the LORD thy God in Horeb in the day of the assembly, saying, Let me not hear again the voice of the LORD my God, neither let me see this great fire any more, that I die not. 17And the LORD said unto me, They have well spoken that which they have spoken. 18I will raise them up a Prophet from among their brethren, like unto thee, and will put my words in his mouth; and he shall speak unto them all that I shall command him. 19And it shall come to pass, that whosoever will not hearken unto my words which he shall speak in my name, I will require it of

him. ²⁰But the prophet, which shall presume to speak a word in my name, which I have not commanded him to speak, or that shall speak in the name of other gods, even that prophet shall die. Deut. 18:14-20

Moses was to be the prototype all the prophets of Israel would follow. All the nations around them had spiritual advisors who were able to make predictions and seek counsel from the demonic realm. The nation of Israel was to be governed by men of God, ordained by God, to speak on behalf of God to the nation.

The ministry of the prophet was established so there would always be a word from God for the people of God. Moses was also letting them know they would ultimately hear from Jesus, who would have a ministry similar to Moses. Jesus would be *the* prophet. Anyone who would not hear Him, it would be required of them. Although he was known as more than a prophet, Jesus was also a prophet. Jesus walked in every office of the five-fold ministry and is the originator of every gift.

Prophetic Authority

> And Elijah the Tishbite, who was of the inhabitants of Gilead, said unto Ahab, As the LORD God of Israel liveth, before whom I stand, there shall not be dew nor rain these years, but according to my word. I Kgs. 17:1

This prophetic declaration set forth by the man of God cannot be reversed by the powers that be. When God established him as his prophet in the land, Elijah was given governmental or prophetic authority over the region of Samaria. Therefore the things which he spoke would come to pass, because God had established him as his prophet.

One of the interesting things about the declaration Elijah made concerning the rain is it was not a "Thus saith the Lord" statement. This statement was made not at the commandment of God, but by the authority given to him by God.

Elijah was known as the prophet of fire. He represented God's spiritual authority in the region of Samaria, where he lived during the reign of Ahab and Jezebel. Ahab was one of the wickedest kings in the Bible.

In the seventeenth chapter of the book of First Kings, Elijah is seen exercising this authority. He decreed it would not rain in Samaria for a certain period of time. Although Ahab was king, his authority did not include the spiritual realm.

Since Elijah was God's prophet in the area, he could engage the spiritual realm under the authority of God. In the sixth chapter of the book of Ephesians, Paul gives us a breakdown of the satanic powers in the second heaven:

> For we wrestle not against flesh and blood, but against principalities, against powers, against the rulers of the darkness of this world, against spiritual wickedness in high places. Eph. 6:12

In this scripture, the kingdom of darkness is broken down by rank and file. Principalities are Satan's generals whom he gives authority over regions. If you notice a particular area or region saturated with a certain vice, this area may be under the influence of a particular principality. In Daniel's day the ruling principality was called the prince of Persia. This principality empowered the Persian people to conquer and rule the known world in his day (see Daniel 10).

Just as the prince of Persia exercised its authority through the Persian Empire, the ruling spirit of Samaria exercised its power through Jezebel. Jezebel was the high priestess for Baal worship. This worship included the use of temple prostitutes and consisted of sexual orgies which made the men in the area weak pawns used at the whim of Jezebel and her followers. Because she had such influence in the community, she usurped the authority of the king, reducing him to a weak figurehead.

Jezebel represented the ruling spirit in the realm of Samaria, and she ruled through manipulation, control and intimidation. Her reign went unchallenged until God raised up the prophet Elijah.

Elijah was a powerful anointed man of God who would resist the powers of Jezebel and turn the people back to God. When Elijah saw the wickedness which was upon the land, he knew he had to confront the evil. He also knew he would incur the wrath of Jezebel while doing it.

If Elijah were to engage the principalities in the region, he had to demonstrate he not only had the power to stop the rain, but also to make the rain return. When the time came for the rain to return, the Lord set the stage for a confrontation which would seal Elijah's authority and set in motion a course of events leading to the end of Jezebel's evil reign in Samaria.

> [1]And it came to pass after many days, that the word of the LORD came to Elijah in the third year, saying, Go, shew thyself unto Ahab; and I will send rain upon the earth. [2]And Elijah went to shew himself unto Ahab. And there was a sore famine in Samaria. I Kgs. 18:1-2

Elijah used the drought and famine to gain the attention of the people of God. It was important for the people of God to realize only the prophet God established had the ability to command the rain to return to the land. The king and the people had to know God alone ruled in the heavens. They had been under the influence of satanic powers for so long, they had forgotten the sovereignty of God.

> ¹⁹Now therefore send, and gather to me all Israel unto mount Carmel, and the prophets of Baal four hundred and fifty, and the prophets of the groves four hundred, which eat at Jezebel's table. ²⁰So Ahab sent unto all the children of Israel, and gathered the prophets together unto Mount Carmel. ²¹And Elijah came unto all the people, and said, How long halt ye between two opinions? If the LORD be God, follow him: but if Baal, then follow him. And the people answered him not a word. ²²Then said Elijah unto the people, I, even I only, remain a prophet of the LORD; but Baal's prophets are four hundred and fifty men. ²³Let them therefore give us two bullocks; and let them choose one bullock for themselves, and cut it in pieces, and lay it on wood, and put no fire under: and I will dress the other bullock, and lay it on wood, and put no fire under: ²⁴And call ye on the name of your gods, and I will call on the name of the LORD: and the God that answereth by fire, let him be God. And all the people answered and said, It is well spoken. I Kgs. 18:19-24

The scriptures above have been among the most preached and written about in the Bible. Men have called it names like the showdown at Mt. Carmel. This was one of the most awesome demonstrations of the power of God and the authority of his prophets in the Bible. Elijah stood alone against over four hundred prophets of Baal.

Notice when Elijah made the challenge the people said it was well spoken. They were not saying they were with him. They were saying he was talking good, but now they wanted a demonstration. This was Elijah's moment to be vindicated in the eyes of man. His authority would no longer be questioned in the area of Samaria. When the fire fell, there would be no one to question whether his authority came from God.

> 40And Elijah said unto them, Take the prophets of Baal; let not one of them escape. And they took them: and Elijah brought them down to the brook Kishon, and slew them there. 41And Elijah said unto Ahab, Get thee up, eat and drink; for there is a sound of abundance of rain. vs 40-41

Elijah had established himself as God's authority in the land. Therefore when he gave the command to destroy the prophets of Baal, the people obeyed. He was letting them know there was a new sheriff in town, and this one had the backing of heaven.

After this great demonstration of power, the people's hearts were prepared for the blessing of rain. Notice how the course of events in these scriptures line up with the word of God.

First you see wickedness in control of the land. This wickedness led to a closed heaven. When the people's hearts were returned to God, He opened the heavens and the rain returned. Even the authority of the prophet must be in line with the word of God. God's word is the final authority in heaven and on earth.

At times when God choses to exercise His authority among the people of God or the priest established by God, he uses the unknown prophets. These prophets show up and declare the sovereignty of God. They usually don't hang around or attempt to make a name for themselves. They don't establish themselves among the powers that be. They're simply God's instruments to declare His judgment:

27And there came a man of God unto Eli, and said unto him, Thus saith the LORD, Did I plainly appear unto the house of thy father, when they were in Egypt in Pharaoh's house? 28And did I choose him out of all the tribes of Israel to be my priest, to offer upon mine altar, to burn incense, to wear an ephod before me? and did I give unto the house of thy father all the offerings made by fire of the children of Israel? 29Wherefore kick ye at my sacrifice and at mine offering, which I have commanded in my habitation; and honourest thy sons above me, to make yourselves fat with the chiefest of all the offerings of Israel my people? 30Wherefore the LORD God of Israel saith, I said indeed that thy house, and the house of thy father, should walk before me for ever: but now the LORD saith, Be it far from me; for them that honour me I will honour, and they that despise me shall be lightly esteemed. 31Behold, the days come, that I will cut off thine arm, and the arm of thy father's house, that there shall not be an old man in thine house. 32And thou shalt see an enemy in my habitation, in all the wealth which God shall give Israel: and there shall not be an old man in thine house for ever. 33And the man of thine, whom I shall not cut off from mine altar, shall be to consume thine eyes, and to grieve thine heart: and all the increase of thine house shall die in the flower of their age. 34And this shall be a sign unto thee, that shall come upon thy two sons, on Hophni and Phinehas; in one day they shall die both of them. 35And I will raise me up a faithful priest, that shall do according to that which is in mine heart and in my mind: and I will build him a sure house; and he shall walk before mine anointed for ever. 36And it shall come to pass, that every one that is left in thine house shall come and crouch to him for a piece of silver and a morsel of bread, and shall say, Put me, I pray thee, into one of the priests' offices, that I may eat a piece of bread. I Sam. 2:27-36

This is a solemn warning delivered by a prophet with no name. His judgment was decreed, because of the wickedness of Eli's sons and how the office of the priest had been diminished. The people had lost respect for the priesthood and the temple. Eli represented God's authority, yet he refused to use this authority to reprimand his sons. He allowed all their ungodly behavior to continue and would not discipline them.

Their practices dishonored God and the temple. Therefore it was the judgment of God they would no longer represent Him as His authority. This judgment did not stop at the house of Eli; it would be a perpetual judgment against the priesthood of Levi.

This prophetic declaration would ultimately open the door for the priesthood as it exists today. It did away with the requirement all priest must be of the lineage of Levi. It also spoke of a new priesthood accountable to God and not man.

In his prophetic decree the prophet declared the Aaronic priesthood would be reduced to shambles. Because of their love for money, they would continuously suffer lack and poverty. Yet in the midst of their failed system, God would establish a new priesthood. This would be an office reserved only for those anointed of God. This priesthood would be an eternal priesthood with Jesus as the high priest forever.

New Testament Prophet

In the New Testament, a change in the ministry of the prophet occurs. Unlike the prophets of old, these men of God were not sent to minister to kings and rulers, but to the emerging church. The final book in the Old Testament is the book of the prophet Malachi, which was followed by four hundred years of silence. It was as if the earth realm was waiting for the prophetic voice to be released from heaven.

During this time of silence, the Hebrew nation had been made subject to the Roman government. The temple had been robbed of its treasures and lost its authority. The priesthood had degenerated into a makeshift marketplace where the people of God were being exploited and oppressed by the very people God chose to shepherd them. If there was ever a need for prophetic guidance, this was the time. Yet there was no voice. The people waited in silence.

During this time of silence the Spirit of God began to move. God heard the prayers of a priest by the name of Zacharias. As he ministered in the temple, he got a word from the angel Gabriel. His wife would have a child. Zacharias and Elizabeth were both beyond the age of child bearing. When she showed up pregnant, everyone wondered what manner of child she would have.

Not much is known about the childhood of John. All that is known is that God released the prophetic voice by the mouth of John when he entered into the ministry.

For the first time in four hundred years the heavens were engaged in spiritual warfare.

> And from the days of John the Baptist until now the kingdom of heaven suffereth violence, and the violent take it by force. Matt. 11:12

Jesus was letting his disciples know they were engaged in violent spiritual warfare.

The warfare he was referring to started as soon as John was born. When Mary found out she was pregnant in the second chapter of Luke, she went to visit Elizabeth and found out she was also about six months pregnant. This makes Jesus and John six months apart. When Herod decreed all male children two years and under would be killed, John's life was also in danger.

This warfare would only escalate as John began to release the prophetic into the atmosphere. It would increase until his life was finally ended at the hand of Herod. His tragic death was proof the spiritual warfare Jesus spoke of was real.

Once the prophetic was released it encountered violent warfare.

The warfare between John and Herod was nothing new. It was like an old song being played over again. If you read the story of Elijah and Ahab and compare it with John and Herod, you will find interesting similarities. Both Ahab and Herod were weak rulers with strong manipulative wives who controlled them and their kingdom. Whereas Jezebel used the temple prostitutes, Herodias used her daughter to control and manipulate Herod.

There is also a unique similarity between Elijah and John. This is one Jesus points out himself:

> [13]For all the prophets and the law prophesied until John. [14]And if ye will receive it, this is Elias, which was for to come. Matt. 11:13-14

The angel Gabriel alluded to this same truth:

> [17]And he shall go before him in the spirit and power of Elias, to turn the hearts of the fathers to the children, and the disobedient to the wisdom of the just; to make ready a people prepared for the Lord. Luke 1:17

Both of these scriptures point to a spiritual connection between John and Elijah. Note also wherever Elijah shows up, Jezebel shows up. This time, she shows up in the form of Herodias, Herod's wife. Whenever these two spirits show up, there is violent warfare.

Although Elijah has the authority to expose and confront Jezebel, he does not have the power to destroy her. This was true in the Old Testament and it is also true in the New Testament. In the Old Testament, it was Jehu who came after Elijah and ultimately destroyed Jezebel. In John's day, it was Jesus who came after John and destroyed Jezebel's power for all time.

Although John was the prophet who ushered in the coming of the

Lord, other prophets, working alongside the apostles, laid the foundation for the New Testament church.

> And are built upon the foundation of the apostles and prophets, Jesus Christ himself being the chief corner stone;

One of these prophets was Agabus, found in the book of Acts:

> 27And in these days came prophets from Jerusalem unto Antioch. 28And there stood up one of them named Agabus, and signified by the Spirit that there should be great dearth throughout all the world: which came to pass in the days of Claudius Caesar. 29Then the disciples, every man according to his ability, determined to send relief unto the brethren which dwelt in Judaea: 30Which also they did, and sent it to the elders by the hands of Barnabas and Saul. Acts 11:27-30

Agabus was a prophet in the New Testament used mightily by God to give direction and guidance to the New Testament church. Agabus also used prophetic acts in his prophecies. In a prophetic act, the prophet uses props to act out his prophecies, signifying what God was doing in the spiritual realm.

> 10And as we tarried there many days, there came down from Judaea a certain prophet, named Agabus. 11And when he was come unto us, he took Paul's girdle, and bound his own hands and feet, and said, Thus saith the Holy Ghost, So shall the Jews at Jerusalem bind the man that owneth this girdle, and shall deliver him into the hands of the Gentiles. Acts 21:10-11

In this prophetic act, Agabus signified Paul would be bound and delivered into the hands of the gentiles. As with the prophets of old, all of his words came to pass just as he said. Paul was bound and taken to Felix, and eventually before Caesar. Just as in the Old Testament, prophets were used mightily of God in the New Testament. Even in today's church, the office of the prophet is still prevalent. As the church grows and claims more territory, this office will continue to grow with it.

CHAPTER FIFTEEN

Evangelist

> But watch thou in all things, endure afflictions, do the work of an evangelist, make full proof of thy ministry.
> 2 Tim. 4:5

> Evangelist -the name given to the NT heralds of salvation through Christ who are not apostles. (G2097)

The office of the evangelist was developed in the New Testament. It consisted of men who were empowered to preach the gospel. Like the apostles, the evangelists traveled to different territories preaching the word. Although they did not operate in the office of the apostle, powerful signs and wonders accompanied their ministries.

If the church is to go forward, the work of the evangelist must continue. Of all the offices of the fivefold ministry, there is none more prevalent than the evangelist. Although all are called into the *work* of an evangelist, not all are called into the *office* of an evangelist. The man or woman who walks in this office is uniquely qualified to teach, preach and demonstrate the power of God.

The evangelist is often thought of as the person who travels to different locations holding meetings and recruiting believers into the body of Christ. Although this is part of the ministry of an evangelist, it is not all inclusive. The evangelist spreads the gospel message, as well as preparing the people to receive Christ. Their job is to go into different areas and prepare the people's hearts for salvation. Their primary responsibility is winning souls for the kingdom of God.

As God's representative, the evangelist is often the first encounter people have with Christ. When he comes to town, it gives the people an opportunity to invite others to church who may not have gone before. There are countless souls in the kingdom of God who never would have gotten saved if someone hadn't invited them to hear an evangelist speak.

When you invite someone to church, you are evangelizing. Some churches have evangelistic teams who go into the community and encourage people to give their lives to the Lord.

Evangelist are usually those who come from the heart of the community. They have a story to tell which compels others to come to Christ.

When Jesus was walking in His earthly ministry, He held evangelistic meetings everywhere He went. As He was evangelizing, He recruited other evangelists to help build the kingdom of God. Oftentimes, He used people with a past to deliver the gospel message. He realized these people would gain the attention of others who were familiar with their story.

Sometimes when people are approached about salvation, they feel as though it is a proposition too much for them to live up to. However, when they know how far someone has been from God and see their lives transformed, hope is renewed in their hearts. This is what happened with the woman at the well.

> [28]The woman then left her waterpot, and went her way into the city, and saith to the men, [29]Come, see a man, which told me all things that ever I did: is not this the Christ? [30]Then they went out of the city, and came unto him. John 4:28-30

After hearing the words of Jesus, this woman was immediately released into her calling and began her ministry as an evangelist.

This woman was an outlier. She lived outside the norm and could not be held down by perceptions of others. She was already despised and lived a socially unacceptable life, so she didn't need the approval of man for her ministry. Unlike many today whose ministries are put on hold as they wait for the approval of man, she went forward in the authority of God. She understood what she received from Jesus was not available anywhere else, and she told others about it. This is what evangelists do. Upon her encounter, she began to walk fully into her ministry as an evangelist.

Although her story is powerful, it is not unique. In the fifth chapter of Mark, we find another person living as an outcast until he meets Jesus:

> 2And when he was come out of the ship, immediately there met him out of the tombs a man with an unclean spirit… 15And they come to Jesus, and see him that was possessed with the devil, and had the legion, sitting, and clothed, and in his right mind: and they were afraid. 16And they that saw it told them how it befell to him that was possessed with the devil, and also concerning the swine. 17And they began to pray him to depart out of their coasts. 18And when he was come into the ship, he that had been possessed with the devil prayed him that he might be with him. 19Howbeit Jesus suffered him not, but saith unto him, Go home to thy friends, and tell them how great things the Lord hath done for thee, and hath had compassion on thee. 20And he departed, and began to publish in Decapolis how great things Jesus had done for him: and all men did marvel. Mark 5:2, 15-20.

This man, who is often referred to as Legion, is not given a name. The demons inside of him said their name was Legion, because they were many. One of the tricks of the enemy is to try to define you by what he does to you. Like many people today, he was known by *what* he was rather than *who* he was. He incited fear in the people around him because his behavior was unpredictable. He spent most of his time in the tombs engaged in self-harming behavior.

On some level, this man realized he was greater than the life he was living. He might not have known how to get out, but he knew Jesus was his way out. When he saw Jesus approaching, he recognized his salvation was nigh. As he approached Jesus, the spirits within him began to protest violently because they knew the man's deliverance was near and they would have to find a new home.

In verse fifteen, the men saw this man's life was transformed. You would think the people would be rejoicing at this amazing deliverance. Instead they're afraid. They had gotten used to seeing him in the condition he was in. This sudden transformation challenged the limits of their perception of him. This, along with the loss of their swine, was too much for them to process. They asked Jesus to depart from them. Imagine for a moment a people so comfortable with bondage they couldn't handle deliverance when it was available.

As Jesus was leaving, the man who had had the legion desired to go with Him, but Jesus told him no. This was unusual. Jesus never turned anyone down who wanted to follow him. I believe the reason Jesus turned him down was because Jesus recognized the man would be more valuable in the ministry if he remained where he was. The man could showcase the power of God to transform lives among those who knew him best.

Upon his deliverance, Jesus appointed the man as an evangelist in his region. Through his testimony and the anointing on his life, this man who was bound by legion was able to bring deliverance to his area. The Bible says he proclaimed the gospel in Decapolis, which means ten cities. As an evangelist, God used him mightily in the same area where he had been oppressed. Jesus knew by their actions the people were not ready for His ministry, but now He had a man in their area and His work could continue.

The first time one hears the office of the evangelist mentioned in the Bible is in Acts 21:8:

> And the next day we that were of Paul's company departed, and came unto Caesarea: and we entered into the house of Philip the evangelist, which was one of the seven; and abode with him.

Although in this scripture Phillip is referred to as an evangelist, he begins his ministry as a deacon:

> 3Wherefore, brethren, look ye out among you seven men of honest report, full of the Holy Ghost and wisdom, whom we may appoint over this business. 4But we will give ourselves continually to prayer, and to the ministry of the word. 5And the saying pleased the whole multitude: and they chose Stephen, a man full of faith and of the Holy Ghost, and Philip, and Prochorus, and Nicanor, and Timon, and Parmenas, and Nicolas a proselyte of Antioch: 6Whom they set before the apostles: and when they had prayed, they laid their hands on them. Acts 6:3-6

Phillip was named a deacon in the early church. When he was ordained, the apostles laid hands on him. This is significant, because it allows you to see the gift of impartation. This might help to explain why Phillip was used so mightily as an evangelist. As he grew in the ministry, he was promoted to the office of an evangelist. Phillip was used extensively of the Lord as he continued to do the work of an evangelist.

26And the angel of the Lord spake unto Philip, saying, Arise, and go toward the south unto the way that goeth down from Jerusalem unto Gaza, which is desert. 27And he arose and went: and, behold, a man of Ethiopia, an eunuch of great authority under Candace queen of the Ethiopians, who had the charge of all her treasure, and had come to Jerusalem for to worship, 28Was returning, and sitting in his chariot read Esaias the prophet. 29Then the Spirit said unto Philip, Go near, and join thyself to this chariot. 30And Philip ran thither to him, and heard him read the prophet Esaias, and said, Understandest thou what thou readest? 31And he said, How can I, except some man should guide me? And he desired Philip that he would come up and sit with him. 32The place of the scripture which he read was this, He was led as a sheep to the slaughter; and like a lamb dumb before his shearer, so opened he not his mouth: 33In his humiliation his judgment was taken away: and who shall declare his generation? for his life is taken from the earth. 34And the eunuch answered Philip, and said, I pray thee, of whom speaketh the prophet this? of himself, or of some other man? 35Then Philip opened his mouth, and began at the same scripture, and preached unto him Jesus. 36And as they went on their way, they came unto a certain water: and the eunuch said, See, here is water; what doth hinder me to be baptized? 37And Philip said, If thou believest with all thine heart, thou mayest. And he answered and said, I believe that Jesus Christ is the Son of God. 38And he commanded the chariot to stand still: and they went down both into the water, both Philip and the eunuch; and he baptized him. 39And when they were come up out of the water, the Spirit of the Lord caught away Philip, that the eunuch saw him no more: and he went on his way rejoicing. 40But Philip was found at Azotus:

and passing through he preached in all the cities, till
he came to Caesarea. Acts 8:26-40

As an evangelist, Phillip understood his first duty was to be obedient to the Holy Ghost. He was instructed where to go by an angel. When he arrived he saw a man reading the scripture. The Holy Ghost instructed him to join his chariot. To be an evangelist, one must be willing to be led fully by the Holy Ghost.

When Phillip recognized the eunuch was in need of ministry, he did what an evangelist does: he led the eunuch to Christ. A good evangelist will never miss an opportunity to lead others to the Lord. Everyone is encouraged to do the work of an evangelist.

Notice what happened after he had baptized the eunuch. He is taken away by the Spirit. This is supernatural and it undoubtedly left an impression on the eunuch he would never forget. Also this is a clear indication of how God uses those in the office of the evangelist. When their job is done in one area, they are moved into another area. Wherever they are, they represent the power of God while they are there.

CHAPTER SIXTEEN
Pastor

> And I will give you pastors according to mine heart, which shall feed you with knowledge and understanding. Jer. 3:15

Of all the offices of the fivefold ministry, the office of the pastor is the most reflective of the heart of God. The relationship between the pastor and the flock is perhaps the most intimate of all. It is the pastor who spends the most time with his flock. His assignment in most cases is as permanent as it gets with ministry. He is there throughout all the stages of their lives. He celebrates their accomplishments as well as mourning their losses. He marries their wed and buries their dead.

The word pastor is derived from the Hebrew word Qal. It means to pasture, tend, graze, or feed. Also shepherd, ruler or teacher (fig). (H7462). In the Greek there are several words used for pastor.

One is aggelos, which means to bring tidings or messenger. This word is also translated angel in the New Testament. (G32). Another word used in the Greek for pastor is poimen (G4166). This word means shepherd or pastor.

The terms "shepherd" and "pastor" are used interchangeably in the New Testament:

> A shepherd in the Near East was responsible for watching out for enemies trying to attack the sheep, defending the sheep from attackers, healing the wounded and sick sheep, finding and saving lost or trapped sheep, loving them, and sharing their lives and to earn their trust. -Vine's Expository Dictionary

In the tenth chapter of the Gospel of John, Jesus gives the model of the Good Shepherd. He asserts there is a marked difference between a shepherd and a hireling. The hireling knows he has a job to do and can be found faithful doing it, but he is only there for the pay. The good shepherd is the one who will lay down his life for the sheep.

> [1]Verily, verily, I say unto you, He that entereth not by the door into the sheepfold, but climbeth up some other way, the same is a thief and a robber. [2]But he that entereth in by the door is the shepherd of the sheep. [3]To him the porter openeth; and the sheep hear his voice: and he calleth his own sheep by name, and leadeth them out. [4]And when he putteth forth his own sheep, he goeth before them, and the sheep follow him: for they know his voice. [5]And a stranger will they not follow, but will flee from him: for they know not the voice of strangers. [6]This parable spake Jesus unto them: but they understood not what things they were which he spake unto them. [7]Then said Jesus

unto them again, Verily, verily, I say unto you, I am the door of the sheep. ⁸All that ever came before me are thieves and robbers: but the sheep did not hear them. ⁹I am the door: by me if any man enter in, he shall be saved, and shall go in and out, and find pasture. ¹⁰The thief cometh not, but for to steal, and to kill, and to destroy: I am come that they might have life, and that they might have it more abundantly. ¹¹I am the good shepherd: the good shepherd giveth his life for the sheep. ¹²But he that is a hireling, and not the shepherd, whose own the sheep are not, seeth the wolf coming, and leaveth the sheep, and fleeth: and the wolf catcheth them, and scattereth the sheep. ¹³The hireling fleeth, because he is an hireling, and careth not for the sheep. ¹⁴I am the good shepherd, and know my sheep, and am known of mine. John 10:1-14

To be a good shepherd, you must enter by the door. This could have several meanings, but the most significant meaning is if you come through the door, you are allowed to come in. This suggests either you have the permission of the owner or the key given by the owner. This fact is important to note because there are other ways to get in. Jesus teaches those who use the alternative ways of entry are robbers and thieves.

No one willingly gives thieves access to their belongings, but a real thief would never consult you for permission to take what belongs to you. He will find another way in. Jesus says "in order to get to my flock you have to come through me."

In the eighth verse of this passage, Jesus makes an important statement:

All that ever came before me are thieves and robbers.

This is important because it sheds light on verse ten. Verse ten is not just talking about the devil. The thief represents anyone who would rob you of a legitimate experience with Jesus. Any time man puts himself before Jesus in your life, you are being robbed. This is the case even if the man is your pastor.

As a good shepherd, you are required to follow Jesus' model but you are not required to be Jesus. "We have these treasures in earthen vessels (II Cor.4:7)", but these vessels come with limitations. There are some things Jesus is able to do but you are not, even if you are willing.

Jesus has reserved a special place in the lives of believers. He will not allow anyone to take His place. The job of the pastor is not to take this place, but to make sure it remains reserved for the one who deserves it.

A good shepherd will recognize danger when it is approaching and warn his flock to preserve their life. He's willing to stand between them and impending harm. This is not the same with a hireling. A hireling is one who is doing what he does only for financial reward. This does not mean he is a bad person. It means his motive is purely financial. It also means he doesn't fit the model of a good shepherd.

A good shepherd is one motivated by his love for the sheep and his commitment to the Lord. He knows he is called and appointed by God to protect and feed the flock, which belongs to God. Although he knows he will be rewarded for his labor, this is not his primary reason for entering the ministry. He knows his reward will be given by God and not man.

Even with this in mind, there will always be those who enter the ministry with hopes of material gain. Their commitment is to this end regardless of what it takes. The word of God gives serious warnings to pastors with the wrong motives:

> [1]Woe be unto the pastors that destroy and scatter the sheep of my pasture! saith the LORD. [2]Therefore thus saith the LORD God of Israel against the pastors that feed my people; Ye have scattered my flock, and driven them away, and have not visited them: behold, I will visit upon you the evil of your doings, saith the LORD. [3]And I will gather the remnant of my flock out of all countries whither I have driven them, and will bring them again to their folds; and they shall be fruitful and increase. [4]And I will set up shepherds over them which shall feed them: and they shall fear no more, nor be dismayed, neither shall they be lacking, saith the LORD. Jer. 23:1-4

Jeremiah gives a stern warning to men who would oppress the people God sent them to liberate. God himself is letting them know there will be a reckoning. He reminds them their responsibility is not only to the people, but the God who called them. Ultimately, they must pay a price for their evildoing and give an account unto God. This is why it is so important for the motives of those who go into ministry to be right. They must know they are called and appointed by God.

When the heart of the pastor is not in sync with the will of God, his motives are determined by fleshly desires. Sometimes these desires will cause him to exploit the people of God. Just as natural relationships can become abusive when love is not the center of the relationship, the same can be the case with spiritual relationships.

The pastor has an awesome obligation to attend to the spiritual needs of the people of God. The authority given by God to pastors brings with it tremendous responsibility. Because of the relationship he has with the members of his flock, they are especially vulnerable to his authority. He must be careful never to violate the trust they place in him. He also needs to be aware it is God who placed him in this position and it is God he must ultimately answer to. Throughout history there have been men who have forgotten this truth, and they've paid an awful price.

Just as the pastor watches over the flock, God is watching over the pastor:

> Feed the flock of God which is among you, taking the oversight thereof, not by constraint, but willingly; not for filthy lucre, but of a ready mind; I Pet. 5:2

Peter reminds the church leaders of his day of their responsibility to the people of God. Again he is warning these leaders their hearts must be pure when it comes to the things of God. The heart of the pastor must always be ruled by love. As he attends to the needs of the people, God will see his needs are met also.

The office of the pastor does not omit him from suffering. There will be times when he will feel as though he is all alone. He will feel like he is there for everyone else, and there is no one there for him. At times like these he must seek God for restoration and refreshing.

Dealing with people is never an easy proposition, even when you are talking about the people of God. Their lives can get messy at times. It is times like these God must be the ruling force in the life of the pastor. God is the only one who can give him the strength he needs to carry on, and he must carry on because his flock is depending on him.

CHAPTER SEVENTEEN
Teacher

But the anointing which ye have received of him abideth in you, and ye need not that any man teach you: but as the same anointing teacheth you of all things, and is truth, and is no lie, and even as it hath taught you, ye shall abide in him. I John 2:27

According to the word of God, the Holy Spirit is the ultimate teacher and guide, responsible for leading us into all truth. Still there are men who walk in the office of the teacher, who spend time in study and communion with God, who are anointed to discover and relate the truth in God's word to other believers. All members of the fivefold ministry are expected to be apt to teach, yet the men who hold the office of the teacher have a special anointing on their lives to impart knowledge of the word of God to other believers.

The ministry of the teacher is perhaps the most needed in the church today. After salvation, the thing most needed is teaching.

Sound doctrine is needed for the new convert as well as those who have been saved for a longer period of time. The one who walks in the office of the teacher must be equipped to deliver the word of God in a way which can stand up to close examination. One who has the reputation of a teacher must therefore be ready to offer clear knowledge concerning the word of God.

This knowledge can only be gained by spending time in the word of God.

> Study to shew thyself approved unto God, a workman that needeth not to be ashamed, rightly dividing the word of truth. II Tim. 2:15

Time spent in the word of God is how the teacher develops his craft. As he spends time in the word, it is the job of the Holy Spirit to give him insight into the deeper things of the Spirit. As a teacher, he has to convey to others what God has revealed to him.

Many times in the word of God Jesus is referred to as teacher or Rabbi. Those in the office of the Rabbi were expected to be effective teachers of the word of God. Some gained reputations as teachers or doctors of the law. These men were considered the final authority in the word of God.

Teachers were always held in high esteem, especially since a large percentage of the population were uneducated at the time. Therefore the people looked to their teachers for wisdom, knowledge, and guidance in the word of God.

> And God hath set some in the church, first apostles, secondarily prophets, thirdly teachers, after that miracles, then gifts of healings, helps, governments, diversities of tongues. I Cor. 12:28

In this scripture, the order is set in establishing the early church. This is not an order based on authority; rather it reflects the order of establishing the church. The churches were established by apostles and prophets. When the churches were in place, a pastor or teacher would be appointed to give instruction and direction to that body of believers. Then those with administrative gifts would get busy establishing church protocol and setting up early churches. As the New Testament church grew, the need for teachers increased proportionately.

The office of the teacher is not a New Testament phenomenon. It was established in the Old Testament. Whenever the people gathered together to hear the word of God, there were teachers appointed to explain and interpret the word for them. These teachers were usually among the tribe of Levi who were set aside for the office of the priest.

> [1]And the Spirit of God came upon Azariah the son of Oded: [2]And he went out to meet Asa, and said unto him, Hear ye me, Asa, and all Judah and Benjamin; The LORD is with you, while ye be with him; and if ye seek him, he will be found of you; but if ye forsake him, he will forsake you. [3]Now for a long season Israel hath been without the true God, and without a teaching priest, and without law. [4]But when they in their trouble did turn unto the LORD God of Israel, and sought him, he was found of them. [5]And in those times *there was* no peace to him that went out, nor to

him that came in, but great vexations were upon all the inhabitants of the countries. ⁶And nation was destroyed of nation, and city of city: for God did vex them with all adversity. ⁷Be ye strong therefore, and let not your hands be weak: for your work shall be rewarded. ⁸And when Asa heard these words, and the prophecy of Oded the prophet, he took courage, and put away the abominable idols out of all the land of Judah and Benjamin, and out of the cities which he had taken from mount Ephraim, and renewed the altar of the LORD, that was before the porch of the LORD.
II Chron. 15:1-8

With the advent of a teaching priest, the people are given instructions and encouragement. Notice the scripture says the Spirit of the Lord came upon the priest as he instructed the people. As I stated earlier, the Holy Spirit is the true teacher. All who walk effectively in the office of the teacher must acknowledge this truth. Without His presence, no teacher would be effective in ministry.

Without the presence of a teaching priest, the people suffered adversity and were vexed in their spirit. This illustrates why the ministry of the teacher is needed in today's church. As they minister to the people of God, the people's faith is increased. They are encouraged to exercise their faith and reach new heights in their personal lives.

As the priest spoke to the people, he spoke words of faith to encourage their hearts and bring them peace. This is what happens when you're in the presence of an anointed teacher. He or she is able to speak the word in a way which brings clarity to life's situations and helps you with your personal struggles.

[1]And all the people gathered themselves together as one man into the street that was before the water gate; and they spake unto Ezra the scribe to bring the book of the law of Moses, which the LORD had commanded to Israel. [2]And Ezra the priest brought the law before the congregation both of men and women, and all that could hear with understanding, upon the first day of the seventh month. [3]And he read therein before the street that was before the water gate from the morning until midday, before the men and the women, and those that could understand; and the ears of all the people were attentive unto the book of the law. [4]And Ezra the scribe stood upon a pulpit of wood, which they had made for the purpose; and beside him stood Mattithiah, and Shema, and Anaiah, and Urijah, and Hilkiah, and Maaseiah, on his right hand; and on his left hand, Pedaiah, and Mishael, and Malchiah, and Hashum, and Hashbadana, Zechariah, and Meshullam. [5]And Ezra opened the book in the sight of all the people; (for he was above all the people;) and when he opened it, all the people stood up: [6]And Ezra blessed the LORD, the great God. And all the people answered, Amen, Amen, with lifting up their hands: and they bowed their heads, and worshipped the LORD with their faces to the ground…[9]And Nehemiah, which is the Tirshatha, and Ezra the priest the scribe, and the Levites that taught the people, said unto all the people, This day is holy unto the LORD your God; mourn not, nor weep. For all the people wept, when they heard the words of the law. [10]Then he said unto them, Go your way, eat the fat, and drink the sweet, and send portions unto them for whom nothing is prepared: for this day is holy unto our LORD: neither be ye sorry; for the joy of the LORD is your strength. [11]So the Levites stilled all the people, saying, Hold your peace, for the day is holy; neither be ye grieved. [12]And all the people went their way to eat, and to drink, and to send portions, and to make great mirth, because they had understood the words that were declared unto them. [13]And on the second day were gathered together the chief of the fathers of all the people, the priests, and the Levites, unto Ezra the scribe, even to understand the words of the law. Neh. 8:1-6, 9-13

When the priest is teaching the people in the scriptures above, he gives them information directly related to their life situation. They gladly received his words because they were able to incorporate them into their everyday lives. They saw the benefits of receiving the words, did exactly as they were instructed, and reaped the results they were expecting. When they put the words they heard in motion, the word was made flesh in them.

Here the people of God are instructed out of the law by the priest and the scribes. These men of God were well-versed in the scriptures and able to give the people an understanding of the scriptures they read. It is obvious they were gifted teachers.

It is stated several different times they made the people understand the law. This is an important gift of the teacher in action. Anointed teachers of the word of God are able to make people understand their teaching. They teach with a clarity able to reach people where they are.

Teachers in the Old and New Testament were also called scribes. The Blue Letter Bible defines scribes as follows:

> [I]n the Bible, a man learned in the Mosaic law and in the sacred writings, an interpreter, teacher. Scribes examined the more difficult and subtle questions of the law; added to the Mosaic law decisions of various kinds thought to elucidate its meaning and scope, and did this to the detriment of religion. Since the advice of men skilled in the law was needed in the examination in the causes and the solution of the difficult questions, they were enrolled in the

Sanhedrin; and are mentioned in connection with the priests and elders of the people. A religious teacher: so instructed that from his learning and ability to teach advantage may redound to the kingdom of heaven. Blue Letter Bible.

The office of the teacher is essential to the fivefold ministry. This office was effective in advancing the kingdom of God. Jesus referred to the scribe in the following parable:

Then said he unto them, Therefore every scribe which is instructed unto the kingdom of heaven is like unto a man that is an householder, which bringeth forth out of his treasure things new and old. Matt. 13:52

In this parable, the scribe is referred to as a householder with treasures old and new. The treasure represents the word of God brought forth in the Old and New Testament. The scribe, or teacher, is able to search the Old Testament scripture, which is filled with types, shadows, and allegories, and apply them to New Testament truths in scripture.

When it comes to teaching the word of God, the biggest mistake you can make is to get before the people and try to impress them with your spirituality or knowledge by using big words. These tactics only illustrate your lack of understanding. The truly gifted teacher is able to relay information in bite-sized morsels everyone can understand and relate to through his or her teaching.

This is why Jesus often used parables in His teachings. The parables bring the teaching out of the rhetorical realm into the world in which the believer lives. When teaching is based on things people can relate to easily, or addresses their needs, it is more readily received.

Although there are many ways in which a preacher or teacher can convey the word of God, there are some significant differences in their approach and delivery of their message. Preaching is to make known the grace of God and the power of the gospel. This is done generally through a broad stroke approach emphasizing an emotional appeal which demands action. Hence preaching is God's chosen method to cause man to realize his need for salvation.

The following scriptures illustrate how God uses the preached word to bring men to salvation. This is the fundamental difference between preaching and teaching.

> [17]For Christ sent me not to baptize, but to preach the gospel: not with wisdom of words, lest the cross of Christ should be made of none effect. [18]For the preaching of the cross is to them that perish foolishness; but unto us which are saved it is the power of God. [19]For it is written, I will destroy the wisdom of the wise, and will bring to nothing the understanding of the prudent. [20]Where is the wise? where is the scribe? where is the disputer of this world? hath not God made foolish the wisdom of this world? [21]For after that in the wisdom of God the world by wisdom knew not God, it pleased God by the foolishness of preaching to save them that believe. I Cor. 1:17-21

The ultimate goal of preaching is to bring men's hearts to repentance. The preached word has the ability to penetrate the hearts of men so they can see the need for salvation. Preaching knocks down walls of resistance and exposes the fallacies of the excuses people offer to keep themselves locked inside the prison of sin.

The real job of preaching after it accomplishes its goal of salvation is to prepare the new convert for teaching to establish him in the kingdom of God. John the Baptist was an anointed preacher of the word of God. He came with a fiery message for the people to "repent for the kingdom of God is at hand (Matt. 3:2)." The Bible says they repented at the preaching of John. When they repented, they were prepared to hear the teaching of Jesus.

Often the record of scripture shows Jesus taught the people before He did miracles. During His teaching, He was building their faith and preparing them to receive the miracles He was about to perform.

When you hear the word preaching, it can bring many different images to mind. These images can vary depending on the denomination, the church culture and the person preaching. Indeed, it is beyond the scope of this book to explore every style of preaching. Yet when you hear the word "teacher", more than likely you imagine someone who facilitates understanding and brings clarity to the word of God.

Teachers are expected to interpret the law of God so man can better understand it. The Old Testament law was given to the priest to help man in his relationship with God and his fellow man. It is through this covenant he better understood the laws of God and the authority to teach the law, which was given to the tribe of Levi.

> [4]And ye shall know that I have sent this commandment unto you, that my covenant might be with Levi, saith the LORD of hosts. [5]My covenant was with him of life and peace; and I gave them to him for the fear wherewith he feared me, and was afraid before my name. [6]The law of truth was in his mouth, and iniquity was not found in his lips: he walked with me in peace and equity, and did turn many away from iniquity. [7]For the priest's lips should keep knowledge, and they should seek the law at his mouth: for he is the messenger of the LORD of hosts. Malachi 2:4-7

The book of Malachi is the last canonized book in the Old Testament. In the passage of scripture above, the Lord is reiterating how he chose the tribe of Levi to minister in the office of the priest. He also states the priest ought to be apt teachers of the word of God. With this great anointing comes great responsibility. The teacher's office is equal to the prophet as well as all the other fivefold ministry gifts. The priest who is teaching is also expected to speak for God as he teaches the word to the people.

Teachers are expected to enhance our understanding of God's word and bring us closer to the Lord. God chose the teaching of His word to cause man to understand His law and His ways:

> He made known his ways unto Moses, his acts unto

the children of Israel. Ps. 103:7

God caused Moses to know His ways so Moses could be an effective teacher for the children of Israel. As a teacher, Moses not only teaches law by precept, but also by example. When he had to deal with a situation, he was expected to deal with it as God would. He was demonstrating God's ways to the people of God.

As leaders in the body of Christ, you have to remember you're always in teaching mode. Your greatest teaching is demonstrated by your actions among the people of God. Your greatest teaching opportunities arise from situations you encounter among the people you minister to. When they see you encounter difficult situations in faith, it increases their faith.

Jesus often took advantage of these opportunities to increase the faith of his followers. When he raised Lazarus from the dead, he purposely waited until he was dead four days. In the Jewish custom, it was a commonly held belief life could come back into the body after three days, but nobody believed this was possible after four days. He knew it would increase their faith if He waited until the fourth day to raise Lazarus from the dead.

This advice is given to teachers by Paul:

> Or ministry, let us wait on our ministering, or he that teacheth, on teaching. Rom. 12:7

Anyone who desires to be an excellent teacher of the word, should be willing to wait. A teacher not only learns in formal settings, but he or she is able to gain insight from life's lessons as well. As he is waiting, he is adding to the well of knowledge he can draw from at any time.

Effective teachers are always in learning mode. They are always learning and therefore always waiting. Just as Jesus waited for the proper time to raise Lazarus from the grave, He is also waiting on the right time to raise you up in your calling.

THE CONCLUSION OF THE MATTER:
Five Fold Ministry

Those who walk in the fivefold ministry enjoy a special place in the body of Christ because of the awesome responsibility they shoulder. As you examine the fivefold ministry, you can compare it to the hand. In effect, it represents the hand of God. It is not a closed fist or an open palm to strike the face of believers, but a hand outstretched to lift up fallen humanity.

Each of the fivefold ministry gifts operates like a finger on the hand of God. The apostle is like the thumb. The thumb is connected to every finger as the apostle often walks in every office of the fivefold ministry. The apostle, like the thumb, is used to gain access to difficult areas and withstand the spiritual challenges of those areas.

The prophet is like the pointing finger. He gives direction to the church when it comes to exploring new areas and opportunities.

The prophet points the way the church should go as he hears and heeds the word of God.

The evangelist is like the middle finger. This is the longest finger on the hand and represents outreach in ministry. Like the middle finger, the evangelist is in the middle of all God would do in the ministry. Like the apostle and prophet, he goes into new areas wherever he is sent to encourage and uplift believers.

The pastor is best represented by the ring finger. His dedication and commitment to the local congregation is like a marriage. In most cases, he is connected to one body of believers for the life of his ministry.

The teacher is represented by the little finger. Although it is small it is essential in the functioning of the hand. It brings stability to the hand as it grasps objects. It is also most closely linked to the ring finger which represents the pastor. This is because these offices are usually held by the same person.

No matter what your calling is in the body, your purpose is the same:

> For the perfecting of the saints, for the work of the ministry, for the edifying of the body of Christ: Eph. 4:12

It is the job of the fivefold ministry to make ready the bride of Christ for His coming.

In this book, I have only touched on a few of the spiritual gifts listed in the Bible. Everyone has a gift. Seek the Lord for your gift. It doesn't have to be a supernatural or fivefold ministry gift. The gift you have uniquely qualifies you for ministry in the kingdom of God.

Whatever your calling, there is plenty of work to be done and time is running out. As you go forward and are faithful in the gift you have, more will be added unto you. God bless you.

Acknowledgements

First, I would like to say thank you to my daughter, Erica Hearns, and Serious Season Publishing. Once again you came through for me. Without your help this effort would have been ordinary at best. You made it exceptional. Thank you for the sacrifices and the countless hours you spent editing, formatting and rearranging this book. I knew what I wanted to say, but you knew how to say it.

Second, I would like to thank the great pastors and church leaders who labored with me and taught me about the word of God. Thank you for your contribution to the pastor and man I have become. Although time would not permit me to name each one of you, there are a couple men of God I feel I owe a special debt of gratitude to, men whose influence profoundly shaped the content of this book and my ministry. I would be remiss if I did not thank Dr. Joseph Fisher, who has mentored me as a Pastor and instructor. I would also like to thank Dr. Don Jones for opening the door to Christian education for me and allowing me to obtain my doctorate degree. The things I learned through the educational opportunities I've been provided with has added an extra dimension to my pastoral ministry.

Most of all, I would like to thank God, who makes all things possible by His Spirit. Thank you, Holy Spirit, the giver of all gifts. Without you, this book, and this life, would not be possible.

About the Author

Dr. Hearns earned his Bachelors of University Studies from the University of Tennessee at Martin. He also earned Bachelors, Masters, and Doctorate degrees from the Midwest College of Theology. Dr. Hearns is the pastor of the Friendly Church of God in Christ in McKenzie, Tennessee. He is also the President and founder of the Adullam Bible College in Gainesville, Florida. Dr. Hearns' publications include *No Lack*, *Cracking the Relationship Code*, and *The Road to Azusa*.

www.ingramcontent.com/pod-product-compliance
Lightning Source LLC
Chambersburg PA
CBHW081146040426
42445CB00015B/1786